JOHN MUIR

To Yosemite
and Beyond

John Muir, 1873. Portrait by Billy Simms, from the files of The Bancroft Library. The original painting is presumably lost. *Courtesy The Bancroft Library.*

JOHN MUIR

To Yosemite and Beyond

Writings from the Years
1863 to 1875

Edited by
Robert Engberg and
Donald Wesling

THE UNIVERSITY OF UTAH PRESS

SALT LAKE CITY

LIBRARY OF CONGRESS CATALOGING-IN-PUBLICATION DATA

Muir, John, 1838–1914
    To Yosemite and beyond : writings from the years 1863–1875 /
John Muir ; edited by Robert Engberg and Donald Wesling.
       p.   cm.
    Originally published: Madison : University of Wisconsin
Press, 1980.
    Includes bibliographical references (p.   ) and index.
    ISBN 0-87480-580-5 (alk. paper)
    1. Muir, John, 1838–1914. 2. Natural history—California
—Yosemite Valley. 3. Naturalists—United States—Biography.
I. Engberg, Robert, 1943– . II. Wesling, Donald. III. Title.
QH31.M9A3 1998
508.794'47—dc21   98-6137

Acknowledgment is made for permission to quote from the following material:

John Muir Papers, Holt-Atherton Department of Special Collections, University of the Pacific Libraries. Copyright 1984 Muir-
Hanna Trust.

"John Muir in Yosemite in 1872." *Sierra Club Bulletin* 23 (1938).

*A Journal of Ramblings through the High Sierra of California by
the University of California Excursion Party*, by Joseph Le Conte.
Reprint, The Sierra Club, 1960.

The Letters of Ralph Waldo Emerson, edited by Ralph L. Rusk,
Volume 6. Columbia University Press, 1939.

Son of the Wilderness: A Life of John Muir by Linnie Marsh Wolfe.
Copyright 1945 by Alfred A. Knopf, Inc. and renewed 1973 by
Howard T. Wolfe. Reprinted by permission of the publisher.

The editors' share in this, John Muir's book,
is dedicated to
Marynell Engberg
and to
Judith, Benjamin, Molly, and Natasha Wesling

Contents

Illustrations

Acknowledgments

Thanks are due to Ross de Lipkau, Muir's heir, for permission to print for the first time certain manuscript materials from the John Muir Papers. Ronald Limbaugh, Archivist at the Holt-Atherton Pacific Center for Western Studies at the University of the Pacific (Stockton, California) literally made this book possible with many professional courtesies. We want also to acknowledge the special help of the following individuals: Robert Hanson at the Yosemite Institute (Yosemite, California); Josephine L. Harper at the State Historical Society of Wisconsin (Madison); Steven Medley at the Yosemite Natural History Association (Yosemite, California). Staff members at the Bancroft Library (University of California, Berkeley), the Huntington Library (San Marino, California), and the University of California, San Diego, have also been helpful to us. Chief Naturalist Jack Gyer showed us the journals and drawings in the Muir Archive of the Yosemite Natural History Association, and gladly supplied us copies. We would also thank Elizabeth Marston Badè, John C. Bell, Michael P. Cohen, Richard Dillon, Sherry Engberg, Charles Ganster, Willis C. Jackman, Marshall S. Kuhn, Roy Harvey Pearce, Kenneth I. Pettit, Nicolos C. Polos, Shirley Sargent, and John Stewart. A portion of Donald Wesling's travel and typing required in the preparation of this book was funded by the Research Committee of the University of California, San Diego. Our gratitude is extended also to Elizabeth Evanson, at the University of Wisconsin Press, for advice and encouragement given us during the final stages of the making of this book.

Preface

This book is a continuation of John Muir's autobiography. After the volumes on his boyhood and youth and on his first summer in the Sierra, he planned to write a book on his Yosemite years, taking his story from 1863 probably to 1875, maybe to 1880. Muir died before he was able to write the book. Our own task has been to try to imagine what his book would have contained. By selecting from his own letters, journals, and articles, we try to give the record of his inner and outer lives during the years after he left the University of Wisconsin. Everything in these writings, as in Muir's experience, either leads up to or away from the ecstatic, central fact of the Yosemite Valley.

The book contains writings of various sorts by Muir from 1863 to 1875. It should be mentioned that this is the first book in the forty years since Linnie Marsh Wolfe edited his journals in *John of the Mountains* (1938) to contain materials taken from Muir's unpublished manuscripts. There is also a selection, in Part III, from biographical writings about Muir by people who met him for the first time in the Yosemite Valley in the years 1870–1872. We have written an interpretive Introduction, along with bridge passages to introduce the selections.

Most books on Muir tend to show Muir as the achieved naturalist, writer, and champion of the wilderness. Instead, we have tried to document his process of self-construction by taking Muir through the struggles of his twenties and thirties. This volume presents Muir's own account of the mind behind the writing and the legend.

R.E. and *D.W.*

San Diego
October 1979

Events in Muir's Life, 1863–1875

1863 John Muir leaves University of Wisconsin for the "University of the Wilderness."

1864 Travels to Canada. Botanizes, begins work in a factory near Georgian Bay.

1865 Remains in Canada, invents new lathing machines for factory. Begins correspondence with Jeanne C. Carr.

1866 Arrives in Indianapolis, works in a machine shop, devises new labor practices. Continues independent science studies.

1867 Nearly blinded by accident to eye; vows to turn from machines and to study nature. Reads first account of Yosemite Valley. Takes one-thousand mile walk to the Gulf of Mexico, writes first journal, nearly dies of a malarial sickness.

1868 Arrives at San Francisco, walks to Yosemite Valley. Spends winter in foothills. First California journals written.

1869 Returns to Yosemite area and spends first summer in the Sierra. Writes journals and notebooks, finds glacial polish: "A fine discovery this." Decides to spend winter in the valley.

1870 Works as sawyer and guide for James Hutchings. Builds cabin near base of Yosemite

1870 (continued)
Falls. Begins study of glaciers. Ecstatic writings in journals. Camps with Joseph Le Conte and the University Excursion Party. Meets Thérèse Yelverton and is included in her novel *Zanita: A Tale of the Yo-Semite*.

1871 Is "more and more interested in science." Guides Boston naturalists around Yosemite. Meets Ralph Waldo Emerson. Concludes Yosemite Creek Basin was carved by glacial erosion; discovers first "living glacier." Publishes first article, "Yosemite Glaciers: The Ice Streams of the Great Valley."

1872 First article published in *Overland Monthly*. Letters published by Boston Society of Natural History. Reveals discovery of "living glaciers." Climbs Mt. Ritter. Spends one week in Oakland, is introduced by Carr as the "wild man of the woods"; flees for Yosemite and writes "A Geologist's Winter Walk."

1873 Year of greatest journal writings. Explores the eastern Yosemite region, Tuolumne, and journeys south to Kings Canyon, climbs Mt. Whitney. Notes the destruction being done to the mountains by sheep and by human "improvements." Begins ten-month "exile" in Oakland, writes series of articles including "Studies in the Sierra."

1874 Returns to Yosemite. Vows to publicize the value of the mountain experience. Begins journeys to northern and southern Sierra. Wonders what is to be the "human part of the mountain's destiny."

1875 Writes for *San Francisco Bulletin*. Expands travels to areas throughout West.

JOHN MUIR

To Yosemite
and Beyond

Introduction

The Emergence of John Muir

> Mr. Muir is a gentleman of rare intelligence, of
> much knowledge of science, particularly of botany,
> which he has made a specialty. He has lived sev-
> eral years in the valley, and is thoroughly ac-
> quainted with the mountains in the vicinity. A man
> of so much intelligence tending a sawmill!—not for
> himself, but for Mr. Hutchings. This is California!
> —Le Conte (1870)[1]

> A "self-styled poetico-trampo-geologist-bot. and
> ornith-natural, etc.!!!"
> —Muir on his profession (1889)[2]

What Muir did and what Muir wrote about represent the beginning of the American conservation movement. He formed for us
the first definition of wilderness, and his work defended and
popularized wild nature.

Muir was born in Dunbar, Scotland, in 1838, and his father,
Daniel Muir, emigrated with the whole family to America when

1. Joseph Le Conte, *A Journal of Ramblings through the High Sierra of
California by the University Excursion Party* (1875; reprint ed., San Francisco:
Sierra Club, 1960), p. 59. The passage was written in 1870.
2. Muir to Robert Underwood Johnson, September 13, 1889, as quoted in
"The Creation of Yosemite National Park," *Sierra Club Bulletin,* 39 (1944): 50.

Muir himself was eleven. From the ages of eleven to twenty-two Muir had no formal schooling, but rather worked his father's farmlands in Wisconsin, which was then at the edge of the frontier. After Muir's woodcarvings and inventions drew attention at a State Fair, he moved to Madison to begin study at the new University of Wisconsin in 1860, and it was at this time he met Mrs. Ezra S. Carr, a professor's wife who became a friend and correspondent. He left the University in 1863 in the middle of the Civil War, without a degree, and spent the next years walking, botanizing, and working in the middle west and Canada. In 1867, nearly blinded by a chance accident in a machine shop where he was working in Indianapolis, he rededicated his life to study. After his eye healed he went on a walking tour which led to the Gulf of Mexico and, eventually, to California by boat and to the Yosemite Valley. From 1868 to 1874 he stayed in or near the Yosemite, working at various jobs to maintain himself, traveling and writing, studying the glaciers and mountains. In 1880 he married Louie Strentzel, settled in Martinez, California, and prospered as a fruit farmer. But there was time for some travel and writing in the 1880s, and by the 1890s he was able to pursue his mountain studies on a nearly full-time basis with the proceeds of his farming. His first books began to appear, he helped found the Sierra Club, and he turned his interest in the wilderness into public activities such as the promotion of a National Parks system and the campaign to preserve Hetch Hetchy Valley. By the time of his death in 1914 he had become a public man, a controversialist, and, not incidentally, a legend: someone less intense than the remote mountaineer of his twenties and thirties, but more human and more significant.

The story of Muir's life has been told many times already: by himself in *The Story of My Boyhood and Youth* and *My First Summer in the Sierra,* by Linnie Marsh Wolfe, by Shirley Sargent, and by a number of recent biographers.[3] The very fact that

3. Most relevant to the present study are Linnie Marsh Wolfe, *Son of the Wilderness: The Life of John Muir* (New York: Knopf, 1945; reprint ed., Madison: University of Wisconsin Press, 1978); and Shirley Sargent, *John Muir in Yosemite* (Yosemite, California: Flying Spur Press, 1971). Still valuable for this period in Muir's life is William Frederic Badè's article "John Muir in Yosemite," *Natural History* 20, no. 2 (1920): 121–41. Other books, theses, chapters, and articles may be found listed in the Selected Readings.

Muir's story contines to fascinate us is itself of interest, suggesting that something about the man and his experience is profoundly representative, profoundly American. Of what, then, is this life the allegory; what does it mean? The answers, we feel, are there in the existing materials, mostly in Muir's own published and unpublished accounts of himself, in a configuration that needs only to be evoked. At the heart of our reading of the life is one dear and culminating place, the Yosemite Valley, and one focal concept, the notion of the wilderness. To reach the full meaning of both Yosemite and the wilderness, we must follow Muir himself and ask how he came to.his special self-definition.

After 1869, the Yosemite Valley was his life's center, its focus, its spiritual home. To Muir, finding this one place was like finding his subject and also, it seems, like finding himself. His life's work expresses itself in movement either away from the valley or in returning to it. Thus, if we want a single phrase to describe his life's meaning and continuity, we might speak of Yosemite as the locale where wilderness shows itself to be the vivid expression of human values. For the biographer, such continuities have their importance. Too often one stage or the other in Muir's life is underplayed; for balance, one should trace lines leading from the younger Muir to the more mature, to the advocate of preserving Yosemite and the wilderness, and finally to the Muir who has become a legend.

The period covered in this book comes after Muir's university years and before he marries. This is, then, the great period which includes his journal of a first summer in the Sierra; his letters to Mrs. Ezra S. Carr, his older friend; his meeting with Emerson; his discovery and proof that the Yosemite was created by glacial gouging; his first articles; and the writing of his first book-length work, *Studies in the Sierra* (not published *as* a book until 1950).

This is the period in which Muir's remarkable intelligence becomes known beyond the circle of family and acquaintances. Le Conte, Yelverton, Emerson, and others who see him in this period, in the midst of his discoveries of self and world, excitedly remark that his intelligence is inspired and inspiring. They see him as a magical person, and they see Yosemite as a special place absorbed into and expressed by a temperament. His portrait is painted and photographed. Muir comes into his own, now, as a scientist (with his glacial theory), and as a writer (with many significant articles published nationally, and the drafting of a book). Also in these years of young manhood Muir makes his personal discovery of the Yosemite, destined to become for others the major locus of American wild nature, but only after the example of his enthusiasm; and Muir discovers his lifework, as by degrees he moves from an elated to an ethical experience of wilderness.

Muir's essential subject was the subject of earlier English writers in his century, and he was especially close in his concerns to the English Romantics and to John Ruskin. He shared with these others a hope that when we describe the world of nature—even in a technological society—we somehow involve ourselves with it so that we may, at best, relate our sense of fact to our sense of value. Nonetheless Muir's version of nineteenth-century landscape engages, as Ruskin's does not, notions of frontier and of wilderness which are specific to American experience.

As the frontier was closed off in the 1880s, and the wilderness of savages and animals and trees was lost, certain aspects of absolute otherness on the American continent were lost.[4] And as one wild thing after another was tamed by the onrush of civilization, lost too was the notion that America could forge a fresh and original accommodation with nature. The pioneers' answer to the threat of the wild prairie was to build cities upon it. The answer to the mild threat of the native Indian was to pen him in reservations, for after all (the reasoning seems to have been) was not the red man something less than human? For when the pioneers saw something different, in people or in landscape, they could not let it alone, they could not study it, they could not honor its separateness.

To the first men on the frontier, fearful of the emptiness, the limitless space, the savagery they witnessed each day, the wilderness was a vast bowl of nothingness that had to be filled.

4. Examples: the great Sioux shaman, Black Elk, was desolated to hear of Mississippi paddleboats whose sole cargo was buffalo tongues; Muir himself was appalled when in 1876 a Sequoia tree was broken apart and reconstructed for the Centennial in Philadelphia.

Even their religion assured them that the earth was theirs to dominate. Nature must be cast out as though it were evil in itself. The wilderness must be colonized both physically and psychologically: physically, by changing its contours to shapes and forms more suitable to man's needs and desires; psychologically, by transforming its absolute otherness into concepts that man could more comfortably accept.

Muir was the first publicly to oppose this belief, and in doing so set the foundation for the American conservationist movement. In a manuscript passage heretofore unpublished, we find Muir arguing against his father's attitude concerning the land and the Indians. We quote at some length, because the passage reveals not only the prevailing ethic of domination, but also Muir's response to it:

> I well remember my father's discussing the Indian Question as to the rightful ownership of the soil, with a Scotch neighbor, a Mr. George Mair. Mr. Mair remarked one day that it was pitiful to see how those unfortunate Indians, children of nature, living on the natural products of the soil, hunting, fishing, and even cultivating small corn fields on the most fertile spots, were now being robbed of their lands and pushed ruthlessly back from their homes into narrower and narrower limits by alien races who were cutting off their means of livelihood until starvation stared them in the face. My father replied, in religious confidence, that it could never have been the intention of God to allow these Indians to ramble over the country, living off game, and keep possession of this fertile soil, which the Scotch and Irish and Norwegian farmers could put to so much better use. Where the Indian requires thousands of acres for his family, these acres in the hands of God-fearing farmers would support ten or a hundred times more people in a worthier and more honorable manner, while at the same time spreading the gospel. Mr. Mair urged that such farming as our first emigrants were practicing was very crude and experimental in many ways: but rude as it was, and ill tilled as were most Wisconsin farms by settlers, many of whom had been merchants and mechanics and servants, how

would we like to have trained specially educated farmers come here and drive us out of our homes and farms, such as they are; making use of the same argument, that God never could have intended such ignorant unprofitable devastating farmers as we were to occupy land upon which scientific farmers could raise five or ten times as much on each acre as we did. No, the Lord intended that we should be driven out by those who could make a right worthy use of the soil. And I well remember thinking that Mr. Mair had much the better side of the argument. It seemed to me then, and does now, that it was simply an example of the rule of might with but little or no thought for the right of the other fellow if weaker; that "they should take who had the power, and they should keep who can," as Wordsworth makes the marauding Scottish Highlanders say. But apart from getting a living, the true ownership of the wilderness belongs in the highest degree to those who love it most. The contemplation of a beautiful landscape excites the highest spiritual pleasure in us, and another and another, and thousands following find and reap crop after crop of this enriching beauty without impoverishing either the landscape, the soil, or his neighbor, and most of the *real* real-estate of the world is of this eternal beauty sort, too often held of no account. Most of our neighbors took up and sweated and grubbed themselves into their graves on a quarter section of land in getting a living and vaguely trying to get rich, while bread and raiment might have been calmly won on a tenth as much with leisure to feed and grow on God's imperishable truth and beauty bread [sic] and lay up treasure in heaven.[5]

The early settlers of the wilderness saw the land solely as a supplier of raw material to be dominated, a producer of wealth to be consumed. Muir's father was one of these first settlers of Wisconsin, typical of other pioneers in the way he exhausted a parcel of land and then moved on to another. Land, wife, even

5. Muir Papers, University of the Pacific, Stockton, California, from Pelican Bay Lodge Manuscript, 1908, File 31.7, pp. 236–39.

children were objects, according to the elder Muir, to be manipulated.

The passage, written in 1908, shows how even as a boy Muir chose to enter the argument on the side of Mr. Mair, rather than to defend his own father. Long before he came to the Yosemite, Muir seems to have had a rather firm notion of how we should treat our natural resources. There is a continuity of thought from the boy in Wisconsin, to the emerging naturalist and writer in Yosemite Valley in the early 1870s, to the old man writing autobiography in these pages of 1908. We cannot treat the emergent, ecstatic man, whose voice we hear in the present book, as the only or best Muir—seeing the older man as losing intensity and selling out to external pressures. But we would be equally wrong if we lost sight of the emergent Muir in our concern for the public or ethical man, the conservationist.

An early, bitter crisis of personality was necessary for those few Americans, like Thoreau and Muir, who managed to live outside the dominant stereotype, outside the belief that nature menaced man. Thoreau and Muir viewed the wild frontier as not so much a place as a state of mind. Their exemplary relation to the natural scene, permitting things to be, even dignifying them as teachers in a university, was something new—an ability to perceive wilderness as value, as ethics, health, discovery, instruction. The irony, of course, is that just as the wilderness is being overrun and dominated, writers begin to see it as threatened potential value; and for the first time in human history make wilderness available for thought.

One of the most revealing human documents of Muir's century is the letter he received from his father, who had just read John's account of his storm night on Mount Shasta. Muir had suffered his father's beatings, had with his brother worked the farm while his father studied the Bible, had had his reading and his inventions censored, had been set to dig a seventy-foot well where he almost died from seeping gas and want of oxygen, had been put on a meatless diet by his father's whim, had later seen his father leave the family in order to preach God's word in faraway cities. The letter stands for these and other indignities, for in it a patriarchal father tries to force a thirty-six-year-old son back into the role of a child by attacking the inner spring of his son's intelligence. The year of the letter is 1874:

My Very Dear John:

Were you as really *happy* as my *wish* would make you, you would be permanently so in the *best* sense of the word. I received yours of the third inst. with your slip of paper, but I had read the same thing in "The Wisconsin," some days before I got yours, and then I *wished* I had not seen it, because it harried up my feelings so with another of your hair-breadth escapes. Had I seen it to be *God's work* you were doing I would have felt the *other* way, but I knew it was not God's work, although you seem to think you are doing God's service. If it had not been for God's boundless mercy you would have been cut off in the midst of your folly. All that you are attempting to show the *Holy Spirit* of God gives the believer to *see* at one glance of the eye, for according to the tract I send you they can see God's love, power, and glory in everything, and it has the effect of turning away their sight and eyes from the things that are seen and temporal to the things that are not seen and eternal, *according to God's holy word.* It is no use to look through a glass darkly when we have the *Gospel* and its *fulfillment,* and when the true practical believer has got the Godhead in fellowship with himself all the time, and reigning in his heart all the time. I know that the world and the church of the world will glory in such as you, but how can they believe which receive honor one of another and seek not the honor that cometh from God only, John 5, 44. You cannot warm the heart of the saint of God with your cold icy-topped mountains. O, my dear son, come away from them to the spirit of God and His holy word, and He will show our lovely Jesus unto you, who is by His finished work presented to you, without money and price. It will kindle a flame of sacred fire in your heart that will never go out, and then you will go and willingly expend it upon other icy hearts and you will thus be blessed infinitely in tribulation and eternally through Jesus

Christ, who is made unto us of God wisdom, righteousness, sanctification, and redemption. I Cor. I, 30, 31. And the best and soonest way of getting quit of the writing and publishing your book is to burn it, and then it will do no more harm either to you or others.[6]

Here the personal attack, which common sense even without the benefit of psychological theory can perceive to be destructive, works under cover of the Biblical rhetoric. We see here hypocrisy, self-justification, megalomania, and all the worst traits of that fundamentalist religion which in its fury to cast out physical nature must also deform all the human nature with which it comes into contact.

The letter may be read as a shorthand for the family situation where John Muir began to be himself. The wonder is not that he survived, for most children do manage to survive, but rather it is the tone and style of his survival of childhood. Many possibilities were doubtless killed off, yet what he was able to make of himself was more resilient and interesting because of the quarrel he had with his father. The quarrel did not break him; living through and beyond the quarrel he was able to become a man.

Daniel Muir's implied utterance to his eldest son was always that the physical world should be loathed, despite its loveliness and bounty. This is the kind of logical and ethical antinomy which can drive a child mad. It did not happen that way, here, for John Muir was able to salvage and foster a selfhood by answering contradictory injunctions with paradoxical statements. Muir did genuinely love his father and never disobeyed him. What he did was to find ways of obeying his father, ways which fulfilled all requests but at the same time transferred a problem back to its originator. For example, Daniel Muir objected to his son's inventions, but could hardly destroy an ingenious clock in the form of a moving scythe which carried the grim biblical reminder that "all flesh is grass" on a written motto. Other inventions such as the early-rising machine (rousing the

6. The letter, headed "Portage City, March 19th, 1874," may be found in William Frederic Badè, *The Life and Letters of John Muir,* 2 vols. (Boston: Houghton Mifflin, 1923–24) 1: 20–23.

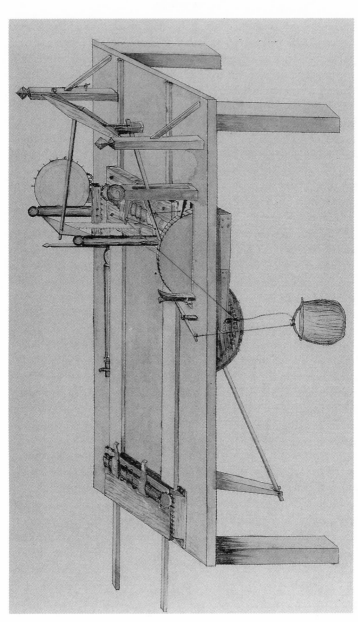

"Self-Setting Sawmill," designed entirely of wood by Muir ca. 1859. Original drawing with the State Historical Society of Wisconsin.

sleeper: good fundamentalist morality), or the revolving study-desk, had always a fanciful, witty possibility which showed the imagination was being indulged—but these items all had an obvious ethical or practical purpose.

In fact, Muir's life and writing are radically displaced versions of evangelical Protestantism. Muir lived outside the stereotypes of his father's Calvinism, but he lived there in ways that are deeply related to it, reversing or exaggerating received attitudes. It is not only that the man who was famous for doing with nothing, or with only bread and tea for days, dies with considerable wealth[7]—but other opposites are resolved in the intellectual shepherd and sawyer, the observer who is not a scientist and the writer who hates to make books, the preacher who is not ordained and who never talks religion, the "athletic philosopher" (Emerson in his description of the American Scholar) who argues that sense-experience can be divine and work can be beauty. Muir is the pilgrim or hermit who, in his lifetime, figures in the national political life. He is the person on the furthest margins—in the wilderness—whose concerns make his message central to a whole historical era, the era of the recession of the wilderness which we still share more than fifty years after Muir's death. His exemplary consistency is really an achieved style of living and writing his self-division.

When Muir began to write in earnest, in the early 1870s, it was necessary to find a way of making a career in research which was, so far as possible, outside the institutions and the positivist definitions of nineteenth-century science; yet also a career which did not violate any of the ethical and religious premises he had absorbed by growing up in his father's house. Muir invented a form of discourse that, as we have said, took all objects of perception as signposts to the eternal. It was a solution to his dilemma of preserving his own meaning while not denying his father's meaning, but a solution that had to be pursued daily in

7. Unknown to his heirs, Muir had large deposits in banks: $179,758 in cash. The rest of the quarter million in assets was made up in this way: ranch $60,000; annual royalties $660; manuscript accepted by publishers $200; 16-acre home $7,000. This information is taken from a newspaper article published shortly after Muir's death: "Muir's Estate Quarter Million," dated January 19, 1915 (no source cited), in file 921, Mu–3, Yosemite National Park Research Library.

perception and through many guises and with a limited literary genre—descriptive prose.

Natura naturans, the informing nature behind physical appearances, is what Muir comes to prize: partly through knowledge of Wordsworth and Ruskin and Emerson and their similar and earlier radical Protestant need for a natural supernaturalism (Carlyle's phrase);[8] partly through what he had learned with his own eyes during his first summer in the Sierra. Muir discovered a way of living in nature which did not understand the world as purely material—a way of moralizing his own observation of the physical world, and this by seeing the Yosemite and its back country and lowlands as if from the aspect of eternity. From this perspective all geologic time is but a day, all the Yosemite region is a book etched in gigantic characters. Time and space are conflated. Continually the reader of Muir has perceptions cleared, as ordinary experience is seen in a new way from a viewpoint which is at once congenial and Olympian, stripping off layers of the real and temporal to show glints of the eternal. Always light is value and transcendence. Always the changeability of the seen, sunrise and sunset, trees against mountain faces, and so on, is the mutable sign of eternal and solemn forms or laws. The "show," as Muir calls it, is grand, but what impels and underlies it is profound.

Muir's tendency, in presenting the world in prose, even in presenting what his father called "another of your hair-breadth escapes," is always to efface himself. It is not obliteration, but the careful pose of an usher: one who takes his experience as in no way unique; one who speaks as the representative of his reader. That voice is an achievement of maturity, and if we hear it properly we hear a voice continuously protecting its utterance from being selfish or thrusting or hectoring in his father's style. There is no wish to dominate the reader and turn the reader into a child. His is a tact, to let the reader alone, based on a larger and finer tact, which is that of letting the natural world alone.

8. M. H. Abrams, in *Natural Supernaturalism: Tradition and Revolution in Romantic Literature* (New York: Norton, 1971), does not once mention John Muir. Nonetheless Muir's descriptive prose is a striking American instance of Abram's very powerful thesis on "the secularization of inherited theological ideas and ways of thinking" (p. 12).

In American society and literature, this letting-alone is a very rare form of good manners, the cosmic tact of a man who has an original relation to the universe. Keats said that which is creative must create itself; Muir had to create his character before and within his writing of the 1870s, performing every new task by the system of avoidance-in-love he had taught himself at the time of his father's earliest beatings. The harshness of the instruction is magnificently met with the gentle resilience of the learner, who can himself go on to teach in more various and subtle ways after he himself, leaving home, leaving formal schooling, has graduated from the university of the wilderness.

When, toward the end of his life, Muir wrote the first section of his autobiography—*The Story of My Boyhood and Youth*— he chose to end the volume at the moment of his leaving the University of Wisconsin. As he described it, this was the moment when he entered the University of the Wilderness. This is a wonderful phrase; it would have been utterly unthinkable a hundred years before Muir's young manhood in the late 1860s and early 1870s; and now, a hundred years later, while it may be more acceptable to us, it is still a dark metaphor. How could the woods, rivers, and mountains be a source and place of higher education?

Muir was greatly influenced, as we have hinted, by the nature-writing of the English Romantics. From them he learned how the outer world, as Wordsworth would have said, tutors us, its pupils.

But Muir made his own American contribution to the ideas of the natural world and to our response to it—human nature itself—a response we might label *wilderness thinking*. Muir, unsystematic but nevertheless emotionally right and complete, left implicit the full explanation of wilderness thinking. Yet all his mature writing returns to and embroiders this theme. To try to work out the meaning of this thinking is to come very close to the center of Muir's life and writings. Yosemite Valley was the university in which he perfected the discipline of such logic, first as the self-taught student and then, increasingly in the 1870s, as the teacher who could put the wilderness into words.

It is our loss that Muir died before extending his autobiography into the years immediately following his first summer in the Sierra. His meditations on this period, from the vantage point of old age, would doubtless have had much to say about how he came into his own self and subject, how he developed a style of being and of writing. However, the passages we do have manage to convey the pattern of his growth into maturity, like a mosaic broken but whole. Most of these passages—from letters, notebooks, and early articles—are written within the 1869–1875 period. Therefore they make up in vivacity what they lack in settled wisdom.

It is possible, too, that Muir completed what he had intended to of his life story. Perhaps leaving this part of the story for last was a deliberate blindness, a recognition that it would have been impossible, or at least very difficult, to render this ecstatic period in after-the-fact language. Or, he may have felt that, after all, he had written about this time of his life in journal articles, and in those books of indirect autobiography, *The Mountains of California* (1894) and *The Yosemite* (1912).

Like most people, Muir survived the trauma of his adolescence—and then forgot about it. But perhaps, with a Calvinist and patriarchal father, he had more than most of us have to survive, more to forget. Long before he was mature as an intelligence or a writer, he was mature as a man; and the oddity of this time lag can probably be traced to the life in his father's house.

This is not the place, nor are adequate concepts at our disposal, for a psychoanalysis of one of the most balanced and productive men of his generation. Yet there remains the need to explain his extraordinary deferral of a choice of life, a seeming aimlessness that lasted until the years 1874–1875. It was plainly a time of ferment, in which the pathological and developmental aspects of his personality were both in evidence. Recent psychology places in adolescence the normative crisis of the whole human life cycle, for the character of adolescence is determined by what went before and also crucially determines much that follows. We have chosen passages in the present book to document the next stage of Muir's life, just after adolescence and his time in the University of Wisconsin. The book shows the length and extraordinary productivity of Muir's time of choosing a lifework; it shows the routes by which his intelligence moved from ecstatic through scientific to ethical awareness, as Muir himself moved from student to teacher in the university of the wilderness.[9]

Muir seems to have lived the years 1869 to 1875 at a continuous pitch of intensity, content at first merely to experience the Yosemite. Then by degrees he felt the need to theorize about his surroundings, to formulate the experience first in journal-books and letters and impromptu talks, then in articles, finally in books. Muir's fiction is that Yosemite taught him wilderness thinking, but of course he brought to the encounter an eager and precise intelligence, one that was well-stored with categories and preconceptions but withal open to the corrections of living. The curriculum of the university of the wilderness during his time there, as one might suspect, was related to the late-nineteenth-century state of knowledge in the natural and human sciences—geology, climatology, botany, glaciology, the physics and aesthetics of travel and survival, the genres of travel narrative and descriptive prose and familiar essay. The lessons were not abstract but practical, growing out of the appropriate meeting of a mind and a terrain.

Muir takes twenty or so years beyond his teens to clear a space for himself, and to marry. The punishing harshness of his background, which he both admits and underplays, eventually results in the judiciousness of his dealings with both humanity and non-human nature. We see him in this period defining life by negation: sampling and then rejecting cities, the society of men and women, and various careers from shepherd and sawyer to tour guide to lecturer and author and professor. He was each of these by turns, but none of these professionally. He became instead, in his own genial and ironic words of 1889, a "self-styled poetico-trampo-geologist-bot. and ornith-natural, etc.!!!"—thus a universalist who comprehends all the specialties, a combined scientist and humanist, someone who sees the world as the field of reconciliation of fact and value. He becomes, in short, a person

9. This account of Muir's young manhood owes much to the formulations of Erik Erikson, particularly to his books titled *Childhood and Society,* 2nd ed. (New York: Norton, 1964), *Young Man Luther* (New York: Norton, 1958), and *Identity: Youth and Crisis* (New York: Norton, 1968).

of pronounced oddity and originality, whose singular angle of approach retains to the end the power to amaze persons who have settled for earlier or lesser definitions of themselves in the world. "The university of the wilderness": such formulations are still provocative.

Muir's young manhood remains of interest precisely because it was not a time of narrowly psychological progress. It was also social and historical. The Muir who eventually emerged became important to his own generation and ours because he had glimpsed an ethics which surpassed technology.

His crisis of career was a choice of not-choosing which lasted inordinately long—through the questioning and demands of family and others who kept urging some kind of settlement. Muir had the tenacity to keep the possibilities open before him as he listened for the voice of a life's work which might say *"This is the real me!"*[10] What he learned in the university of the wilderness corresponded to no category in the existing range of careers available in his America. So he held on until he could invent a life and career along paths he would blaze for himself. To do this was to enact wilderness thinking first of all in his own life; the books came later. In view of what happened in the 1890s, when he became a national figure, his time spent earning money in the 1880s appears not a diversion but just another stage in preparing for what he had to do: teach wilderness thinking.

In his own life between 1869 and 1875, the wilderness had the function of a university because it permitted him the freedom to sample several possibilities, to range over physical terrains and mental disciplines, to try his powers, to resist the process whereby individuality is standardized. The sheer sensuality of the experience, a passion different from that of physical love but no less intense, was also a factor: pain and pleasure of the body, and of the eye; measures by the body's faculties of endurance,

10. Muir's contemporary William James, who like Muir prolonged this time of career choice beyond all the normal limits of their century, speaks of the moment of decision when one's true work can begin: "A man's character is discernible in the mental or moral attitude in which, when it came upon him, he felt himself most deeply and intensely active and alive. At such moments there is a voice inside which speaks and says 'This is the real me!'" Quoted in Erikson, *Identity: Youth and Crisis*, p. 19.

the body's dimensions. "X-rays of beauty that get into one thru bones and flesh": that, from an unpublished note, is the essential Muir speaking.[11] Modern backpackers feel especially close to this language of bodily elation; Muir gives in striking anecdotes and images the human glory of drifting along in a physical world. The best lesson of the wilderness, on this showing, is that it reduces to a proper perspective what is most trivial and personal in personality.

To Muir for one, then, to call something wild was to render it the highest praise. To label a stream or mountain peak wild was to join in harmony the non-human world of nature with the conscious experience of man. For Muir, one aspect of intelligence can find its birth in wilderness experience. Muir knew what his journeys in the Yosemite region had accomplished for him, and he recognized the virtue of such trips for all persons, in the cleansing power they would effect. At the same time, Muir did not attack civilization—he merely defended the wilderness in its richest potential for man.

The belief was reflected in his style, the narrative form in which his words come to us. While Muir is the first-person-singular hero of all his narratives, his presence does not intrude on the scene. Nature is the real subject, the character he is trying to develop. Muir himself, always present, remains in the background, sharing his observations but taking none of the attention away from the true subject of his discourse.[12]

Wilderness thinking is exploration beyond the reaches of the conventional, the movement from the known to the wild, culture to nature. Earthquake and avalanche, grizzly bear and rattlesnake, were not for Muir threats against his superior selfhood, but rather the most dramatic instructors in the university of the wilderness. These, along with sunset, alpenglow, massing clouds, waterfall-mist, aurora borealis, windstorm, snow ban-

11. Muir Papers, File 37.14, Autobiographical Fragments, n.d., handwritten copy: Muir's notes as transcribed by Linnie Marsh Wolfe.
12. Several of the points in this and the previous paragraph are ably treated in Michael P. Cohen's 1973 dissertation, whose title, "The Pathless Way," beams a welcome light on Muir's sense of wilderness as innovative possibility. See Cohen, "The Pathless Way: Style and Rhetoric in the Writing of John Muir," Ph.D. diss., University of California at Irvine, 1973.

ner, forest fire, were really nature's aesthetic media, each evoking its own elated tone of consciousness. "This grand show," he said, "is eternal."[13] To know nature's scenes without fear is, for Muir, to learn new possibilities for the self. For the city-dwelling modern person, harnessed to clock-time, these scenes would create a renewal because they make real to our senses that our body is "a sponge steeped in immortality . . . and represents an acceptance of immortality in the world."[14] Between the lines of some of his letters to his son, Daniel Muir rightly understands the challenge of John's heretical, Romantic doctrine of immanence to his own transcendental Calvinism. And yet John Muir, schooled in his father's Scottish rigor, would never present wilderness as mere aesthetic self-indulgence. "One must labor," he said, "for beauty as for bread, here as elsewhere."[15] His statement is at once a radical redefinition of the nature of the wilderness, the category of the aesthetic, and the force of human labor.

Here, then, are the reasons why Muir reigns as Elder of the Tribe of conservationists, why his part in the mountain's destiny is that of founder, exemplary spokesman. Here, too, is the material to tell us that the years up to 1875 led Muir, step by step, to the attitudes and actions of the busy years that followed. Here, likewise, we can detect the roots of the ethical concerns that first appeared in the 1860s, but developed into the mature concepts of Muir's later years.

John Muir lived in, and in part created, a historical moment when humanistic studies were not entirely separable from the natural sciences. Always he valued the experiential over the mediated, or the written; and yet always he was drawn to the ways of mediation. "A physical fact," he noted as a college freshman in 1861, "is as sacred as a moral principle."[16] Perhaps because he took this notion with him to Yosemite, most physical

13. Quoted in Linnie Marsh Wolfe, ed., *John of the Mountains: The Unpublished Journals of John Muir* (Boston: Houghton Mifflin, 1938; reprint ed., Madison: University of Wisconsin Press, 1979), p. 438.
14. In Cohen's fine words ("The Pathless Way," p. 146), which echo Muir's own words of the 1870s.
15. From Chapter 1 of *The Yosemite* (New York: Century, 1912; reprint ed., Garden City, N.Y.: Doubleday, Anchor Books, 1962), p. 20.
16. Quoted in Wolfe, *Son of the Wilderness*, p. 132.

facts are morally individuated in Muir's writings, as experience is harvested and interpreted. Ecstatic science and ecstatic writing sooner or later become elements of wilderness thinking. When Muir's writing arcs back to his own genuine experience, it is always and equally looking ahead to the personal experience of the reader. And so Muir presses his materials, whether these be human studies or nature studies, toward the sacredness of physical fact, changing everything by his wilderness ethics.

He is of the first rank neither as a scientist nor as a writer, not a Darwin nor a Tennyson, but he is someone perhaps equally as rare: an intellectual worker who, working out from the stable center of his own perceptions, is able to use both forms of inquiry to make a new kind of intelligence.

Leaving the Yosemite after meeting Muir in 1871, Emerson said: "There is a young man from whom we shall hear." Muir was then totally unknown, yet on his return to Concord, Emerson inscribed Muir's name last on a short list of great names titled "My Men." People were often having this sense of revelation about young Muir. In a letter to Muir from Mrs. Carr, received just before his departure for California, she says: "[God] gave you the eye within the eye, to see in all natural objects the realized ideas of His mind. . . . He will surely place you where your work is."[17] Mrs. Galloway, in conversation with Muir, remarks: "Well, John, my dear laddie, your day will never be done. There is no end to the kind of studies you are engaged in, and you are sure to go on and on."[18] And of course they were right—or rather Muir made them right. "I might have become a millionaire," Muir wrote, thinking of his success in the factories, "but I chose to become a tramp!"[19] There was a decisiveness not only in the choice of life, but in the later understanding and acceptance of that choice. "I have lived a bully life. I have done what I set out to do."[20] Those are the words of someone whose work was his life.

17. Quoted in Wolfe, *Son of the Wilderness,* pp. 104–5.
18. Quoted in Badè, *Life and Letters,* 1: 156.
19. Quoted in Wolfe, *Son of the Wilderness,* p. 110.
20. John Muir, quoted in Edwin Way Teale, ed., *The Wilderness World of John Muir* (Boston: Houghton Mifflin, 1954), Introduction, p. xx.

In honoring that sense of accomplishment, it is well to remind ourselves of Muir's special late-nineteenth-century time of commercial and technological expansion: the time in which he decided not to become a millionaire. The best of recent commentators on life history and the historical moment remarks usefully that "it is only in periods of marked transition that the innovators appear: those too privileged in outlook to remain bound to the prevailing systems; too honest or too conflicted not to see the simple truths of existence hidden behind the complexity of daily 'necessities'."[21] Muir lived in a moment of a new dominant class of specialists in university and in industry, those who know what they are doing; but it was also the time of an intense new group of universalists, those who mean what they are saying. The interplay between the two groups will determine the possibilities for identity in a given historical setting. Muir, in our reading at least, is very lonely in his time and place in the way he combines at the highest level aspects of the whole range from specialist to universalist. Scientist and humanist, athletic philosopher, he both knows what he is doing and means what he is saying.

Muir's emergence is a primary nineteenth-century instance of an intelligence unifying itself against the odds of family and historical matrix, so to stand against that "conspicuous, energetic, unmixed materialism" which, Muir himself said, "rules supreme in all classes."[22] There is the spectacle of a whole man moving within a divided culture. Muir's was a new kind of life, a projection of the possible in the 1870s. We see such persons more often now, and rightly so, because (as Mrs. Galloway said) there is no end to the kind of studies he was engaged in.

21. Erik Erikson, *Identity: Youth and Crisis,* p. 32. From Erikson is also derived this paragraph's notion that the interplay between specialists and universalists determines the possibility for identity in a given period.
22. Quoted in Wolfe, *Son of the Wilderness,* p. 131.

Part One

To Yosemite (1863–1869)

Not like my taking the veil—no solemn abjuration of the world. I only went out for a walk, and finally concluded to stay out till sundown, for going out, I found, was really going in.

Muir, *John of the Mountains*, 1913(?)

John Muir often spoke of his arrival in Yosemite as the result of "fate and flowers"—as the culmination of both inner will and outer fortune. Into a small hand-sewn notebook written sometime in the late 1870s he recalled the events and decisions which had finally led him to the valley. He remembered feeling tormented after his university years, as friends and family pressured him to settle down—he wrote it "settle *down*"— and cautioned him to select a career, perhaps even choose a bride, while all along he wished for the freedom to explore and continue the studies begun at the university.

One by one he denied each profession as it was suggested to him. He sold the poor land deeded him by his father, knowing doubtless it was insufficient ever to sustain a farm; he rejected the ministry, telling a friend he would be more tempted to preach nature's ways than those of the conventional church, and anyway his own faith, as he told close friends, was growing weak; and he abandoned medicine even before commencing its study, choosing instead to wander off to Canada rather than enroll in the Ann Arbor School of Medicine. The inventions and the whir of machines held him the longest, from his stay in Canada to the eye-injury in Indianapolis, yet from these too he turned—not because they made him unhappy (he was "always happy in the center" he once wrote), but because they could not put out the "restless fires" he felt within.

Four years after leaving the university came the accident to the eye, in March 1867, and when he recovered he said good-bye to friends and family and began his thousand-mile walk to the Gulf of Mexico. So began a planned three-year saunter in which he would, he thought, walk south and eventually raft down the Amazon. Written in his familiar handwriting across the top of an autobiographical manuscript dictated by him in 1908 (the "Pelican Bay Lodge Manuscript") are the words "First Vol. after leaving University—Canada and Florida."* Evidently this period of his life was to be given a separate volume of his autobiography. It would come after his *Boyhood and Youth* (completed 1913) and would itself be followed by one or two other volumes dealing with his California and Yosemite years. His death in 1914 ended the plan.

* The "Pelican Bay Lodge Manuscript" exists as some 500 type-written pages transcribed from a stenographer's notes taken from Muir's dictation while he was at E. H. Harriman's Oregon retreat during the summer of 1908. Muir later used the first portion of these notes for *The Story of My Boyhood and Youth* (Boston: Atlantic Monthly Co., 1913; reprint ed., Madison: University of Wisconsin Press, 1965); the other pages he revised but did not work into autobiographies. Portions have been printed in William Frederic Badè, *Life and Letters of John Muir* 2 vols. (Boston: Houghton Mifflin, 1923–24) and in Linnie Marsh Wolfe, *Son of the Wilderness: The Life of John Muir* (New York, 1945; reprint ed., Madison: University of Wisconsin Press, 1978). The complete typescript is now with the Muir Papers at the University of the Pacific, Stockton, California.

Nonetheless it is possible to take direction from his notes and journal comments, and to present those discoveries of self and nature which he probably wished to include in these uncompleted autobiographies; included here are the portions of both published and unpublished manuscripts which we believe would have formed the core of his narratives.

The story begins in 1863 as Muir says farewell to the University of Wisconsin. He was far from satisfied with what he had taught himself while a student, yet he sensed it was time to move on. In the closing paragraph of *The Story of My Boyhood and Youth* he writes:

From the top of a hill on the north side of Lake Mendota I gained a last wistful, lingering view of the beautiful University grounds and buildings where I had spent so many hungry and happy and hopeful days. There with streaming eyes I bade my blessed Alma Mater farewell. But I was only leaving one University for another, the Wisconsin University for the University of the Wilderness.

The Story of My Boyhood and Youth (Boston: Atlantic Monthly Co., 1913; reprint ed., Madison: University of Wisconsin Press, 1965), p. 228.

———————

In an unpublished portion of the Pelican Bay Lodge Manuscript Muir recalled why he left.

Anyway I quietly walked off without saying anything about a diploma, and eagerly entered the University of the Wilderness. Many years later the University sent me the honorary degree of Doctor of Laws, in recognition of my contributions to science and the work I had done in the cause of Forestry out in this western country; not, however, until a year after Harvard had recognized my work and conferred the honorary degree of A.M. I left the University without the slightest thought of making a name, but urged on and on in search of beauty and knowledge. Away I wandered happy and free and poor into the glorious American wilderness.

Muir Papers, University of the Pacific, Stockton, California, File 31.7, Pelican Bay Lodge Manuscript, p. 165.

———————

The following passage we take from Muir's hand-sewn notebook, a collection of autobiographical notes and thoughts written probably in 1878. Clearly the phase of his life after leaving the university and before finding the Yosemite was a painful one; the selection shows that he was constantly worried about how and when he would conform to society's ways. Muir struggled with the options open to him and finally, we discover, he chose *not* to make a choice—instead to grant himself a three-year sabbatical in the woods, where he would saunter, collect his thoughts, and study. What follows is doubtless the most central of all documents for the understanding of the young man Muir.

From the date of my arrival in the American wilderness my walks with nature have been interrupted by only 4 years of university study and the odd times taken up in earning a livelihood. Shortly after leaving college I began to doubt whether I was fully born. Past all controversy I was *on* the world but was I really *in* it. I was tormented with that soul-hunger of wh' we hear so much nowadays, that longing and vague unrest regarded as proof of immortality. This was the time too when all the world is said to lie before us for choice, when armed with small bits of lessons from school and church we are to be the architects of our own fortunes, build our existences as a carpenter a house, hack and hew and make hard concious efforts as we go, add this and that by dint of sheer (unsunned, unnourished) ignorant will. A few friends kindly watched my choice of the half dozen old ways in which all good boys are supposed to walk. "Young man," they said, "choose your profession—Doctor, Lawyer, Minister?" "No, not just yet," I said.

My student days seem likely to be my best and should be prolonged. Accordingly, leaving books and life plans and all the beaten Charts of the religious believer, and fortunes from here to heaven, I went strolling off into the woods botanizing,* wandering at will in bog and meadow, along stream banks, in flat Illinois prairies and in pine and hemlock woods around the Great Lakes, the great sky over me, sauntering free and alone in a continued state of [manuscript blurred]. The beauty and harmony of sunshine and crystal water filled every faculty with intense joy. How beautiful and fresh and Godful the world began to appear. The only exception to complete contentment was the lingering notion instilled from childhood that I had work to do as part of society. I must choose a profession and settle down,

---

* The manuscript is not clear here. Perhaps Muir's meaning is: "Accordingly, leaving my books and life-plans and all the conventional paths from here to heaven, I went strolling off into the woods botanizing. . . ."

stand still and be a pillar in family, at school, or such like in a
church. But Nature held me afield. I lingered in woods and bogs
in pursuit of science. Botany and geology led me on, or rather I
allowed those sciences to pursue me, for though I studied hard,
all kinds of wild beauty was allowed to come in me, to draw and
hold me as they were able. Some five years spent themselves thus
when the friendly admonition I began to consider seriously concerning so-called life-work. I would be a physician or inventor
and "settle down," a dreadfully significant term, settling *down,*
and should not be done rashly. It should be done with ceremony
and religious rites. About this time it occurred to me that it
would be a fine thing to make and take one more grand Sabbath
day three years long (but how long should it be, 1-2-3 summers)
during which I would go botanizing in tropic lands and woods,
thus accumulating a stock of wild beauty, landscapes with their
flowers and light sufficient to lighten and brighten my afterlife in
the shadows of civilization's defrauding "duties." Accordingly
feeling free and conscience calm again I bade farewell and
entered at once upon the enjoyment of my three year's *Sun*day.
With a plant press and small satchel on my back I was ready, visions of tropic lands made me rich.

Muir Papers, File 40.2, "Hand-Sewn Notebook," pp. 2–5.

The following letter, printed here for the first time, reveals Muir's
uneasiness about his weakening Christian faith and the fear he might
not choose the proper paths in life. The letter is addressed to Ambrose
Newton, whom Muir had met while a student at Wisconsin, and ex-
plains that a draft lottery delayed his departure for the Ann Arbor
School of Medicine. His name was not drawn, yet unexplainably Muir
decided not to enroll in medical school and within the next few months
he was in Canada, where he was to remain for the next three years.

Fountain Lake
February 16, '64

Dear friends:

It was with real pleasure that I received your long good letter
yesterday so full of the experience and fruit of the aged Christian. I was sorry to think that it had been so long a time in the office, but I shall hereafter be more careful about my mail. A draft
was being made just when I should have been starting for Ann

Arbor which kept me at home, but letters addressed to Midland shall always reach me wherever I am.* I was happy to perceive in your letter so much of that quiet resignation which the true living Christian can feel under all of the afflictions which may be placed in his cup. How dreadful must be the conditions of those who, when called to pass through the same bitter waters of sorrow, have no heavenly arm to rest upon—all human aid so utterly powerless, and can look for none from God. How greatly we should prize and love that gospel which shows us the hand of a kind Heavenly Parent directing all the good and ill that makes life the changeful and mysterious thing which it is.

One of our neighbors must be borne to the grave tomorrow— a Christian who long has known the power of a Saviour's love. She died in hope of the glory of God about to be revealed to her. Like summer plants the most sainted believer sickens and dies, but thanks be to God for the Gospel which proclaims immortality for those cold limbs about to be folded in the coffin.

I sometimes fear that I am not prepared to die at any time, —that I do not keep the shortness and uncertainty of life sufficiently in view, and it seems too that I do not think enough of heaven as a reality. I have faith but surely it is weak: for I do not find these unseen realities in my everyday thoughts and plans. Were I sure that in a few years I should go to France and that I might be taken there at any time, I am sure that it would exert a controlling influence upon all of my plans; but here in a city whose maker and builder is God—Heaven in whose length and breadth not a mortal or unholy thing is found, —to this place I admit and claim that at any time I may be removed, and still, strange to say, I almost forget it in seeking a path through the world. Again when I reflect upon the magnitude of life's duties, and upon the numberless paths which lead astray, and feel at the same time that I am so susceptible of bad impressions, I think of the lines which begin thus

> "O fear not thou to die,
> But rather fear to live."

My sheet I see is nearly full and I must close. I am really happy, Mr. Newton, to think of having you as a correspondent.

* Muir's name was evidently not drawn in the draft lottery.

I have many friends but none so aged and experienced as yourself. I feel that I have need of the advice and counsel of Chris-
tians. I am sure I shall always give your letters a heart's welcome.
I thank you for the expressions of esteem which you have
tendered me in your kind letter but feel that I do not deserve
them.

Remember me with much respect to your partner, and may
you always be cheered and upheld by the God of all consolation.

Goodbye.

Muir Papers, Correspondence, Box 14, Letters Sent, 1860–1873.

The months after his departure from the University of Wisconsin found
Muir at home in Portage, working part-time at the family farm and
spending other weeks botanizing with friends. Sometime during this
period he heard the news that the Peltons' infant, Fannie, had died at
age twenty months. The following letter, which we reproduce exactly,
was sent to console them, and even in its syntax shows Muir to be profoundly shaken. The Peltons had befriended him during his brief stay at
Prairie du Chien in 1860, and here he struggles to write of his profound
sorrow.

Fannie is dead O God what can I say, or what can I do.
Well well do I know how little letterfulls of condolence can do
here. Your little blessing is away but—Oh Mr. and Mrs. Pelton you know Jesus loves the little dear, and all is well. And
you'll go to her in just a little while though she cannot come
to you. blessed blessed will you be if washed by Jesus' blood
you be found sinless as she. Love Jesus the more. He knows
the strength of this woe. Think how many dangers and aches
your little dear has been spared by leaving a little earlier than
yourselves. And she is safe, all safe and all blessed.

If in death still lovely—

lovelier THERE, far lovelier

You know how sorely I feel this myself and how deeply I sympathize with you, I'd better say no more.

"Jesus died"

JOHN—

State Historical Society of Wisconsin, Madison, SC185, "Letters and Poems, 1861–1914,
written by John Muir to Emily Pelton and her mother, Mrs. F. N. Pelton of Prairie du
Chien, Wis."

While a student at the university Muir had often visited the home of Professor and Mrs. Ezra S. Carr. Mrs. Carr was to become a close friend and advisor during the ensuing years of Muir's young manhood. Their letters to each other, warm and personal, at times suggest that only the strict mores of their century, and Muir's shy nature, were keeping the pair from developing a romantic attachment. These letters, many of which are reproduced in this book, gave Muir a link to ordinary reality and permitted him to share his enthusiams and discoveries with a sympathetic audience.

The following letter is the first of the series, and was written while Muir was living in Canada. Clearly, Muir's restlessness was continuing. He tells Mrs. Carr of his resolve to study, to explore, and to "be a Humboldt."

Trout's Mills, near Meaford [Canada]
September 13*th* [1865]

Dear Mrs. Carr:

Your precious letter with its burden of cheer and good wishes has come to our hollow, and has done for me that work of sympathy and encouragement which I know you kindly wished it to do. It came at a time when much needed, for I am subject to lonesomeness at times. Accept, then my heartfelt gratitude— would that I could make a better return.

I am sorry over the loss of Prof. Sterling's letter, for I waited and wearied for it a long time. I have been keeping up my irregular course of study since leaving Madison, but with no great success. I do not believe that study, especially of the Natural Sciences, is incompatible with ordinary attention to business, still, I seem able to do but one thing at a time. Since undertaking, a month or two ago, to invent new machinery for our mill, my mind seems to so bury itself in the work that I am fit for but little else; and then a lifetime is so little a time that we die ere we get ready to live.

I would like to go to college, but then I have to say to myself, "You will die ere you do anything else." I should like to invent useful machinery, but it comes, "You do not wish to spend your lifetime among machines and you will die ere you do anything else." I should like to study medicine that I might do my part in lessening human misery, but again it comes, "You will die ere you are ready to be able to do so." How intensely I desire to be a Humboldt! but again the chilling answer is reiterated. Could we but live a *million* of years, then how delightful to spend in perfect contentment so many thousand years in quiet study in college, so many amid the grateful din of machines, so many among human pain, so many thousands in the sweet study of Nature among the dingles and dells of *Scotland,* and all the other less important parts of our world! The *perhaps* might we, with at least a show of reason, "shuffle off this mortal coil" and look back upon our star with something of satisfaction.

I should be ashamed—if shame might be in the other world—if any of the powers, virtues, essences, etc., should ask me for common knowledge concerning our world which I could not bestow. But away with this *aged* structure and we are back to our handful of hasty years half gone, all of course for the best did we but know all of the Creator's plan concerning us. In our higher state of existence we shall have time and intellect for study. Eternity, with perhaps the whole unlimited creation of God as our field, should satisfy us, and make us patient and trustful, while we pray with the Psalmist, "So teach us to number our days that we may apply our hearts unto wisdom."

I was struck with your remarks about our real home as being a thing of stillness and peace. How little does the outer and noisy world in general know of that "real home" and real inner life! Happy indeed they who have a friend to whom they can unmask the workings of their real life, sure of sympathy and forbearance!

I sent for the book which you recommend. I have just been reading a short sketch of the life of the mother of Lamartine. These are beautiful things you say about the humble life of our Saviour and about the trees gathering in the sunshine.

What you say respecting the littleness of the number who are called to "the pure and deep communion of the beautiful, all-loving Nature," is particularly true of the hard-working, hard-drinking, stolid Canadians. In vain is the glorious chart of God in Nature spread out for them. So many acres chopped is their motto, so they grub away amid the smoke of magnificent forest trees, black as demons and material as the soil they move upon. I often think of the Doctor's lecture upon the condition of the different races of men as controlled by physical agencies. Canada, though abounding in the elements of wealth, is too difficult to subdue to permit the first few generations to arrive at any great intellectual development. In my long rambles last summer I did not find a single person who knew anything of botany and but a few who knew the meaning of the word; and wherein lay the charm that could conduct a man, who might as well be gathering mammon, so many miles through these fastnesses to suffer hunger and exhaustion, was with them never to be discovered. Do not these answer well to the person described by the poet in these lines:

> "A primrose by the river's brim,
> A yellow primrose was to him,
> And nothing more."

I thank Dr. Carr for his kind remembrance of me, but still more for the good patience he had with so inapt a scholar. We remember in a peculiar way those who first give us the story of Redeeming Love from the great book of revelation, and I shall not forget the Doctor, who first laid before me that great book of Nature, and though I have taken so little from his hand, he has at least shown me where those mines of priceless knowledge lie and how to reach them. O how frequently, Mrs. Carr, when lonely and wearied, have I wished that like some hungry worm I could creep into that delightful kernel of your house—your library—with its portraits of scientific men, and so bountiful a store of their sheaves amid the blossom and verdure of your little kingdom of plants, luxuriant and happy as though holding their leaves to the open sky of the most flower-loving zone in the world!

That "sweet day" did, as you wished, reach our hollow, and another is with us now. The sky has the haze of autumn and, excepting the aspen, not a tree has motion. Upon our enclosing wall of verdure new tints appear. The gorgeous dyes of autumn are too plainly seen, and the forest seems to have found out that again its leaf must fade. Our stream, too, has a less cheerful sound and as it bears its foam-bells pensively away from the shallow rapids in the rocks it seems to feel that summer is past.

You propose, Mrs. Carr, an exchange of thoughts, for which I thank you very sincerely. This will be a means of pleasure and improvement which I could not have hoped ever to have been possessed of, but then here is the difficulty: I feel that I am altogether incapable of properly conducting a correspondence with one so much above me. We are, indeed, as you say, students in the same life school, but in very different classes. I am but an alpha novice in those sciences which you have studied and loved so long. If, however, you are willing in this to adopt the plan that our Saviour endeavored to beat into the stingy Israelites, *viz.* to "give, hoping for nothing again," all will be well, and as long as your letters resemble this one before me, which you have just written, in genus, order, cohort, class, province, or kingdom, be assured that by way of reply you shall at least receive an honest "Thank you."

Tell Allie* that Mr. Muir thanks him for his pretty flowers and would like to see him, also that I have a story for him which I shall tell some other time. Please remember me to my friends, and now, hoping to receive from you at least *semi-occasionally,* I remain,

Yours with gratitude,
JOHN MUIR

William Frederic Badè, *The Life and Letters of John Muir,* 2 vols. (Boston: Houghton Mifflin, 1923–24), 1:139–44.

The following year Muir left Canada for Indianapolis, judging that it would have factories and employment opportunities, and "with the advantage of being in the heart of one of the very richest forests of deciduous hard wood on the continent."† Muir found a job in one of the mills there, and soon was making labor-saving devices and recommending a reformation of the assembly procedures. In March of 1867 came the accident, which Muir described in a portion of his autobiographical manuscript published in William Frederic Badè's *Life and Letters.*

A serious accident hurried me away [from Indianapolis] sooner than I had planned. I had put in a countershaft for a new circular saw and as the belt connecting with the main shaft was

---

* One of Mrs. Carr's sons.
† Badè, *Life and Letters,* 1:153.

new it stretched considerably after running a few hours and had to be shortened. While I was unlacing it, making use of the nail-like end of a file to draw out the stitches, it slipped and pierced my right eye on the edge of the cornea. After the first shock was over I closed my eye, and when I lifted the lid of the injured one the aqueous humor dripped on my hand—the sight gradually failed and in a few minutes came perfect darkness. "My right eye is gone," I murmured," closed forever on all God's beauty." At first I felt no particular weakness. I walked steadily enough to the house where I was boarding, but in a few hours the shock sent me trembling to bed, and very soon by sympathy the other eye became blind, so that I was in total darkness and feared that I would become permanently blind.

When Professor Butler learned that I was in Indianapolis, he sent me a letter of introduction to one of the best families there, and in some way they heard of the accident and came to see me and brought an oculist, who had studied abroad, to examine the pierced eye. He told me that on account of the blunt point of the file having pushed aside the iris, it would never again be perfect, but that if I should chance to lose my left eye, the wounded one, though imperfect, would then be very precious. "You are young and healthy," he said, "and the lost aqueous humor will be restored and the sight also to some extent; and your left eye after the inflammation has gone down and the nerve shock is over-come—you will be able to see about as well as ever, and in two or three months bid your dark room good-bye."

So I was encouraged to believe that the world was still to be left open to me. The lonely dark days of waiting were cheered by friends, many of them little children. After sufficient light could be admitted they patiently read for me, and brought great handfuls of the flowers I liked best.

As soon as I got out into Heaven's light I started on another long excursion, making haste with all my heart to store my mind with the Lord's beauty and thus be ready for any fate, light or dark. And it was from this time that my long continuous wanderings may be said to have fairly commenced. I bade adieu to all my mechanical inventions, determined to devote the rest of my life to the study of the inventions of God. I first went home to

Wisconsin, botanizing by the way, to take leave of my father and mother, brothers and sisters, all of whom were still living near Portage. I also visited the neighbors I had known as a boy, renewed my acquaintance with them after an absence of several years, and bade each a formal good-bye. When they asked where I was going, I said, "Oh! I don't know—just anywhere in the wilderness southward. I have already had glorious glimpses of the Wisconsin, Iowa, Michigan, Indiana and Canada wildernesses; now I propose to go south and see something of the vegetation of the warm end of the country, and if possible wander far enough into South America to see tropical vegetation in all its palmy glory."

All the neighbors wished me well and advised me to be careful of my health, reminding me that the swamps in the south were full of malaria. I stopped overnight at the home of an old Scotch lady who had long been my friend, and was now particularly motherly in good wishes and advice. I told her that as I was sauntering along the road near sundown I heard a little bird singing, "The day's gone, The day's done." "Well, John, my dear laddie," she replied, "your day will never be done. There is no end to the kind of studies you are engaged in, and you are sure to go on and on, but I want you to remember the fate of Hugh Miller." She was one of the finest examples I ever knew of a kind, generous, great-hearted Scotchwoman.

After all the good wishes and good-byes were over, and I had visited Fountain Lake and Hickory Hill* and my first favorite gardens and ferneries, I took a thousand-mile walk to the Gulf of Mexico from Louisville, across Kentucky, Tennessee, North Carolina, Georgia, and Florida.

Badè, *Life and Letters*, 1:154–56.

———————

Muir evidently intended to make the story of his trip south one of the chapters, or segments, in his autobiography. He may well have planned on using the journal he kept during this saunter—a journal which he revised in later life and which was published after his death as *A Thousand-Mile Walk to the Gulf* (1916). His autobiographical notes of

* Muir's two boyhood homes, near Portage, Wisconsin.

these months are brief; we give here the narrative as it appears in the
Pelican Bay Lodge Manuscript.

Here [in Florida] I was taken down with malarial fever, which
kept me about three months in Cedar Keys, Florida. Then I
sailed for Cuba, where I botanized for a month or two. Thence I
intended going to South America, along the Andes, from the
north end of the Continent until I struck a tributary of the
Amazon, where I intended to make a raft or skiff and float down
to the Atlantic; but finding that I was convalescing but slowly,
and that so long a tropical trip was likely to lead through sickly
places, I thought that I had better postpone the South American
excursion and go to healthy California to see its Yosemite and
the Big Trees and wonderful wild flora in general. Accordingly,
going to New York on a schooner loaded with oranges I there
took passage on a steamer sailing for Panama, crossed the
Isthmus, and arrived in San Francisco in April; stayed one day in
San Francisco and then inquired of a man, who was carrying
some carpenter's tools, the nearest way out of town to the wild
part of the State. He in wonder asked "Where do you wish to
go?" "Anyplace that is wild;" so he directed me to the Oakland
ferry, saying that would be as good a way out of town as any.
Leaving the train at East Oakland I took the first road I came to
and walked up the Santa Clara Valley. The Oakland hills at this
time (April) after a very rainy season were covered with
flowers—beds of yellow and blue and white in endless variety
made the slopes of the hills seem like a brilliant piece of patch-
work, while the air was quivering with sunshine and lark song.
     Passing through San Jose and on to Gilroy, I began to inquire
the way to Yosemite, and was directed to cross the coast range
by the Pacheco Pass.

Muir Papers, File 31.7, Pelican Bay Lodge Manuscript, pp. 177–78.

———————————

Muir walked towards Yosemite with a shipboard friend named
Chilwell. Their general plan was to find the way to the Merced River,
which Muir knew drained Yosemite, then follow it up to the valley.
Muir's account of this first encounter with the Sierra has remained little
known. Yet it deserves to be read both as example of Muir's wit and

good humor and as correction to the view that he always traveled alone and unarmed. We take up the narrative as the pair reaches Pacheco Pass.*

At the top of the Pass I obtained my first view of the San Joaquin plain and the glorious Sierra Nevada. Looking down from a height of fifteen hundred feet, there, extending north and south as far as I could see lay a vast level flower garden, smooth and level like a lake of gold—the floweriest part of the world I had yet seen. From the eastern margin of the golden plain arose the whole Sierra. At the base ran a belt of gently sloping purplish foothills lightly dotted with oaks, above that a broad dark zone of coniferous forests, and above this forest zone arose the lofty mountain peaks, clad in snow. The atmosphere was so clear that although the nearest of the mountain peaks on the axis of the range were at a distance of more than one hundred and fifty miles, they seemed to be at just the right distance to be seen broadly in their relationship to one another, marshaled in glorious ranks and groups, their snowy robes so smooth and bright that it seemed impossible for a man to walk across the open folds without being seen, even at this distance. Perhaps more than three hundred miles of the range was comprehended in this one view.

Descending the pass and wading out into the bed of golden compositae five hundred miles long by forty or fifty wide, I found that the average depth of the vegetation was over knee-deep, and the flowers were so crowded together that in walking through the midst of them and over them more than a hundred were pressed down beneath the foot at every step. The yellow of these compositae, both of the ray and disc flowers, is extremely deep and rich and bossy, and exceeds the purple of all the others in superficial quantity forty or fifty times their whole amount. But to an observer who first looks downward, then takes a wider and wider view, the yellow gradually fades, and purple predominates, because nearly all of the purple flowers are taller.

* An expanded account—perhaps the one Muir intended to use in his autobiography—appears in "Rambles of a Botanist among the Plants and Climates of California," *Old and New* 5 (June 1872): 767–72.

In depth, the purple stratum is about ten or twelve inches, the yellow seven or eight, and down in the shade, out of sight, is another stratum of purple, one inch in depth, for the ground forests of mosses are there, with purple stems, and purple cups. The color-beauty of these mosses, at least in the mass, was not made for human eyes, nor for the wild horses that inhabit these plains, nor the antelopes, but perhaps the little creatures enjoy their own beauty, and perhaps the insects that dwell in these forests and climb their shining columns enjoy it. But we know that however faint, and however shaded, no part of it is lost, for all color is received into the eyes of God.

Crossing this greatest of flower gardens and the San Joaquin River at Hill's Ferry, we followed the Merced River, which I knew drained Yosemite Valley, and ascended the foothills from Snelling by way of Coulterville. We had several accidents and adventures. At the little mining town of Coulterville we bought flour and tea and made inquiries about roads and trails, and the forests we would have to pass through. The storekeeper, an Italian, took kindly pains to tell the pair of wandering wayfarers, new arrived in California, that the winter had been a very severe one, that in some places the Yosemite trail was still buried in snow eight or ten feet deep, and therefore we would have to wait at least a month before we could possibly get into the great valley, for we would surely get lost should we attempt to go on. As to the forests, the trees, he said, were very large; some of the pines eight or ten feet in diameter.

In reply I told him that it would be delightful to see snow ten feet deep and trees ten feet thick, even if lost, but I never got lost in wild woods. "Well," said he, "go, if you must, but I have warned you; and anyhow you must have a gun, for there are bears in the mountains, but you must not shoot them unless they come for you and you are very, very close up." So at last, at Mr. Chilwell's anxious suggestion, we bought an old army musket, with a few pounds of quail shot and large buckshot, good, as the merchant assured us, for either birds or bears.

Our bill of fare in camps was simple—tea and cakes, the latter made from flour without leaven and toasted on the coals—and of course we shunned hotels in the valley, seldom indulging even

Yosemite Valley (1868). Oil painting by Albert Bierstadt. Collection of the Oakland Museum of California, Gift of Miss Marguerite Laird in memory of Mr. and Mrs. P.W. Laird.

in crackers, as being too expensive. Chilwell, being an Englishman, loudly lamented being compelled to live on so light a diet, flour and water, as he expressed it, and hungered for flesh; therefore he made desperate efforts to shoot something to eat, particularly quails and grouse, but he was invariably unsuccessful and declared the gun worthless. I told him I thought that it was good enough if properly loaded and aimed, though perhaps sighted too high, and promised to show him at the first opportunity how to load and shoot.

Many of the herbaceous plants of the flowing foothills were the same as those of the plain and had already gone to seed and withered. But at a height of one thousand feet or so we found many of the lily family blooming in all their glory, the Calochortus [Mariposa Lily] especially, a charming genus like European tulips, but finer, and many species of two new shrubs especially, Ceanothus and Adenostoma. The oaks, beautiful trees with blue foliage and white bark, forming open groves, gave a fine park effect. Higher, we met the first of the pines, with long gray foliage, large stout cones, and wide-spreading heads like palms. Then yellow pines, growing gradually more abundant as we ascended. At Bower Cave on the north fork of the Merced the streams were fringed with willows and azalea, ferns, flowering dogwood, etc. Here, too, we enjoyed the strange beauty of the Cave in a limestone hill.

At Deer Flat the wagon-road ended in a trail which we traced up the side of the dividing ridge parallel to the Merced and Tuolumne to Crane Flat, lying at a height of six thousand feet, where we found a noble forest of sugar pine, silver fir, libocedrus, Douglas spruce, the finest of the world, towering in all their unspoiled beauty and grandeur around a sunny, gently sloping meadow. Here, too, we got into the heavy winter snow—a fine change from the burning foothills and plains.

Some mountaineer had tried to establish a claim to the Flat by building a little cabin of sugar pine shakes, and though we had arrived early in the afternoon I decided to camp here for the night as the trail was buried in the snow which was about six feet deep, and I wanted to examine the topography and plan our course. Chilwell cleared away the snow from the door and floor of the cabin, and made a bed in it of boughs of fernlike silver fir, though I urged the same sort of bed made under the trees on the snow. But he had the house habit.

After camp arrangements were made he reminded me of my promise about the gun, hoping eagerly for improvement of our bill of fare, however slight. Accordingly I loaded the gun, paced off thirty yards from the cabin, or shanty, and told Mr. Chilwell to pin a piece of paper on the wall and see if I could not put shot into it and prove the gun's worth. So he pinned a piece of an envelope on the shanty wall and vanished around the corner, calling out, "Fire away."

I supposed that he had gone some distance back of the cabin, but instead he went inside of it and stood up against the mark that he had himself placed on the wall, and as the shake wall of soft sugar pine was only about half an inch thick, the shot passed through it and into his shoulder. He came rushing out, with his hand on his shoulder, crying in great concern, "You've shot *me,* you've shot *me,* Scottie." The weather being cold, he fortunately had on three coats and as many shirts. One of the coats was a heavy English overcoat. I discovered that the shot had passed through all this clothing and into his shoulder, and the embedded pellets had to be picked out with the point of a penknife. I asked him how he could be so foolish as to stand opposite the mark. "Because," he replied, "I never imagined the blank gun would shoot through the side of the 'ouse."

We found our way easily enough over the deep snow, guided by the topography, and discovered the trail on the brow of the valley just as the Bridal Veil came in sight. I didn't know that it was one of the famous falls I had read about, and calling Chilwell's attention to it I said, "See that dainty little fall over there. I should like to camp at the foot of it to see the ferns and lilies that may be there. It looks small from here, only about fifteen or twenty feet, but it may be sixty or seventy." So little did we then know of Yosemite magnitudes. *

After spending eight or ten days in visiting the falls and the high points of view around the walls, making sketches, collecting flowers and ferns, etc., we decided to make the return

* The fall is nearly 900 feet high.

trip by way of Wawona, then owned by Galen Clark, the Yosemite pioneer.

From Pelican Bay Lodge Manuscript, in Badè, *Life and Letters,* 1:180–88.

"Oh, no, not for me," Muir remembered was his thought upon first seeing the Yosemite Valley. Into an autobiographic notebook he wrote of finding the Yosemite too large, too deep, too incomprehensible for human understanding.* Evidently he was satisfied that his visit should last only a week or so. He was not yet looking for what he saw—and so he left the valley, and Clark's, and arrived at Snelling, on the San Joaquin plain, where he found work as a field hand, ferryman, and finally as a shepherd for a man known locally as "Smoky Jack."

While the journal of his first Yosemite trip has not been found, other extant notebooks and letters give some idea of his thoughts and moods during this period in the foothills. The following letter he sent to his brother David a few weeks after arriving at Snelling.

> On Merced river near Snelling
> Merced Co., Cal., July 14th [1868].

Dear Bro. David,

I have lived under the sunny sky of California nearly 3½ months, but have not yet rec'd a single letter from any source— perhaps a few went to the dead letter off[ice] while I was in the mountains, but I am settled now with a ranchman for eight or nine months and hope to enjoy a full share of the comfort of letters during my long isolation.

I traveled along the San Jose valley from San Fran. to Gilroy and crossed the Diabolo Mountains by the Pacheco pass, crossed the plains and river of the San Joaquin, and traveled on into the Sierra Nevadas to the mammoth trees and magnificent Yo Semite Valley, thence down the Merced to this place.

My health, which suffered such wreck in the South, has been thoroughly patched and mended in the mountains of California. I had a week or two of fever before leaving the plains for Yo Semite, but it was not severe, and I was only laid up three or four days, and a month in the Sierra cooled with mountain winds and delicious crystal water has effected a complete cure.

And now Davie, this is splendid country, and one might

---

* Muir Papers, University of the Pacific, Stockton, California, File 70.12, Muir Autobiographical Notes.

Notebook page from "Smoky Jack's Sheep Camp," written in 1869 while Muir lived near Snelling, California. Notebook No. 9165, page 21. John Muir Papers, Holt-Atherton Department of Special Collections, University of the Pacific Libraries. Copyright 1984 Muir-Hanna Trust.

truthfully make use of more than half of the Methodist hymn "Land of pure delight" in describing it, and it flows with more of milk and more of honey than ever did old Canaan in its happiest prime. Of all the bright shining ranks of happy days that God has given me since I left Wisconsin, these of California are the happiest.

This place is ten or a dozen miles from the lowest foothills of the great Sierra range, and opposite and parallel to it at the distance of 40 or 50 miles is the Diabolo range, both of which with their gorges, and valleys, and sharp snow-clad peaks, are in full clear view, like a picture in a room. They form, together with the purple plains and pure sky, a source of exhaustless and unmeasurable happiness from all the fields where I work.

I have been in the harvest field, but harvest work is easy here where headers are used. Many farmers in this valley raise from 10 to 20 bushels of grain. I never had so easy times in harvest field before. I worked for some time here at the wild and novel business of sheep-shearing, and had very funny, lawless, exciting times. There were about thirty men in the first gang I worked in, composed of Spanish, Indian, Irish, English, Scottish, and mixed, mongrel, unanalyzable elements of California society "too numerable to mention." All of this pied regiment in driving the sheep into the shearing pens would hoot and yell like demons. The sheep, wild as antelopes, would become ungovernable, and a sort of wholesale sheep hunt would commence in which deeds of romantic daring might be witnessed in the heaving, surging masses of men and mutton equal to those of the knights of old in tournament. These sheep are not like those of Palestine—dumb before their shearers, for many of them keep up wild and obstreperous warfare with kick and bleat, from the first snip at ears to the last at tail.

My love to Cath [Catherine Merrill] and the little ones. Please write very soon, and advise Maggie [Margaret Muir] and J[ohn]. Reid and all the rest to write.

Affectionately,
J. M.

Send my letters to Hopeton. It is nearer than Snelling.

Muir Papers, Correspondence, Box 14, Letters Sent 1860–1873.

In another letter to his brother Daniel we learn that Muir's inner conflict over a choice of career was continuing. He was still uneasy about his life, and told his brother he wished to stop all the wandering (which had carried him some six thousand miles during the previous twelve months) and settle somewhere, at least for awhile. Yet in the same note he confessed his belief that he might never be able to settle down and conform—might always be separated from the great mass of mankind and from the normal modes of thinking.*

Muir's earliest California journal dates from this period spent near the Sierra foothills. The first few pages are given below, and they reveal that Muir, tired of the traveling and the "sabbatical" he had undertaken, had decided to give up the nomadic life, and would remain in California.

[December, 1868]

Since coming to this Pacific land of flowers I have walked with Nature on the sheeted plains, along the broidered foothills of the great Sierra Nevada, and up in the higher piney, balsam-scented forests of the cool mountains. In these walks there has been no human method—no law—no rule. A strong butterfly full of sunshine settles not long in any one place. It goes by crooked unanticipated paths from flower to flower. Sometimes leaving blossoms of very taste, it alights in the mud of a stream, or glances up into the shadows of high trees, or settles on loose sand or bare rock. Such a life has been mine, every day and night of last summer spent beneath the open sky; but last month brought California winter and rain, so a roof became necessary, and the question came, What shall I do? Where shall I go?

I thought of the palmy islands of the Pacific, of the plains of Mexico, and of the Andes of Peru, but the attractions of California were yet stronger than all others, and I decided to stay another year or two.

Linnie Marsh Wolfe, ed., *John of the Mountains: The Unpublished Journals of John Muir* (Boston: Houghton Mifflin, 1938; reprint ed., Madison: University of Wisconsin Press, 1979), p. 2.

---

* The Huntington Library, San Marino, California, File FAC 625, Letter to Daniel Muir, April 17, 1868.

Muir spent the fall and winter as a shepherd, watching the seasons progress, and recording his observations in his journal.* They were lonely months, yet also among his happiest.

January 1, 1869

The New Year was ushered in with rain, a black day without a single sunbeam. The purple and brown colors are fast fading from the plains, the bright youthful plant green is deepening with astonishing rapidity. Every groove and hollow, however shallow, has its stream—living water is sounding everywhere. 'Tumbling brown, the burn comes down, and roars from bank to brae.' I celebrated the Happy New Year crossing countless streams, running 'ower moor and mire through gude and gide' in full chase of the wretched sheep.

Everything is governed by laws. I used to imagine that our Sabbath days were recognized by Nature, and that, apart from the moods and feelings in which we learn to move, there was a more or less clearly defined correspondence between the laws of Nature and our own. But out here in the free unplanted fields there is no rectilineal sectioning of times and seasons. All things *flow* here in indivisible, measureless currents.

January 22 [1869]

Light southeast wind. Clouds transparent veils. Hoar-frost. The larks this morning sang to the words 'We'-ero spe'-ero we'-eo we'-erlo we'eit.' I wish I could understand lark language.

Dreamed in the sunbeams, when the sheep were calm, the plan of a hermitage: walls of pure white quartz, doors and windows edged with quartz crystals, windows of thin smooth sheets of water with ruffling apparatus to answer for curtains. The door a slate flake with brown and purple and yellow

---

* These journals form Chapter I of Linnie Marsh Wolfe, ed., *John of the Mountains: The Unpublished Journals of John Muir* (Boston: Houghton Mifflin, 1938; reprint ed., Madison: University of Wisconsin Press, 1979) For a further account of Muir's life in the foothills, see his "Twenty Hill Hollow," *Overland Monthly* 9 (July 1872): 80–86. This same article he later revised, and Badè used it as Chapter 10 in his edition of *A Thousand-Mile Walk to the Gulf* (Boston: Houghton Mifflin, 1916), pp. 192–212.

Dry creek on whose 25 happy bank my cabin stands is subject to sudden swellings & overflows in the rainy winter season when it becomes a majestic stream almost a river with serious & confident gestures, curving about its jutting banks & horseshoe bends carrying fences & bridge timbers & all careless logs & houses within reach of its ephemeral power In the few hours course of a after the close of a rain it will retire within its to its narrow beaten path leaving many flat smooth fresh sheets of sand. I like to watch the first writings upon these great new made leaflets of Nature's own making One of these pages was made last night & was already written upon when I saw it this morning. It is

"Smoky Jack's Sheep Camp," page 25. John Muir Papers, Holt-Atherton Department of Special Collections, University of the Pacific Libraries. Copyright 1984 Muir-Hanna Trust.

lichens. And oh, could not I find furniture! My table would be a grooved and shinning slab of granite from the bed of the old mountain glaciers, my stool a mossy stump or tree bracket of the big dry, stout kind, and a bed of the spicy boughs of the spruce, etc., *ad infinitum*.

January 31.

Nature's fields are fully green from mountain range to mountain range over all the plains. The late rains have made many shallow pools, and this evening they are noisy with a musical population. An immense crop of batrachians have come to life more suddenly than mushrooms. Where have all these frogs been during the long dry season?

My sheep are long-legged and long-tailed, and come in gallant style from the hillsides when pursued by my two dogs. Today I observed one of the sheep inquisitively smelling and examining a large hare. The hare allowed the sheep to touch him with his nose.

Without question this has been the most enjoyed of all the Januarys of my life.

Wolfe, ed., *John of the Mountains*, pp. 8, 17, 21.

During 1868 Professor Carr left the University of Wisconsin after a dispute over curriculum and financing. He moved his family to Oakland, where he became one of the first professors at the new State University of California (University of California). Mrs. Carr wrote to Muir and he responded with the following letter, expressing his joy that he might find a friend in California. The letter also shows him stubbornly unwilling to descend, at this time in his life, "from the clouds and flowers to the practical walks of politics and philanthropy."

Near Snellings, Merced Co., [Cal.]
February 24th, 1869

Your two California notes from San Francisco and San Mateo reached me last evening, and I rejoice at the glad tidings they bring of your arrival in this magnificent land. I have thought of you hundreds of times in my seasons of deepest joy, amid the flower purple and gold of the plains, the fern fields in gorge and

cañon, the sacred waters, tree columns, and the eternal un-
nameable sublimities of the mountains. Of all my friends you are
the only one that understands my motives and enjoyments. Only
a few weeks ago a true and liberal-minded friend sent me a large
sheetful of terrible blue-steel orthodoxy, calling me from the
clouds and flowers to the practical walks of politics and
philanthropy. Mrs. Carr, thought I, never lectured thus. I am
glad, indeed, that you are here to read for yourself these glorious
lessons of sky and plain and mountain, which no mortal power
can ever speak. I thought when in the Yosemite Valley last
spring that the Lord had written things there that you would be
allowed to read some time.

I have not made a single friend in California, and you may be
sure I strode home last evening from the post office feeling rich
indeed. As soon as I hear of your finding a home, I shall begin a
plan of visiting you. I have frequently seen favorable reports
upon the silk-culture in California. The climate of Los Angeles is
said to be as well tempered for the peculiar requirements of the
business as any in the world. I think that you have brought your
boys to the right field for planting. I doubt if in all the world
man's comforts and necessities can be more easily and abun-
dantly supplied than in California. I have often wished the
Doctor near me in my rambles among the rocks. Pure science is a
most unmarketable commodity in California. Conspicuous,
energetic, unmixed materialism rules supreme in all classes.
Prof. Whitney, as you are aware, was accused of heresy while
conducting the State survey, because in his reports he devoted
some space to fossils and other equally dead and un-California
objects instead of columns of discovered and measured mines.

I am engaged at present in the very important and patriarchal
business of sheep. I am a gentle shepherd. The gray box in which
I reside is distant about seven miles northwest from Hopeton,
two miles north of Snellings. The Merced pours past me on the
south from the Yosemite; smooth, domey hills and the tree
fringe of the Tuolumne bound me on the north; the lordly
Sierras join sky and plain on the east; and the far coast mountains on the west. . . .

My most cordial regards to the Doctor. Californians do not deserve such as he.

A lawyer by the name of Wigonton or Wigleton, a graduate of Madison, resides in Snellings. I suppose you know him.

I am your friend,
JOHN MUIR

John Muir, *Letters to a Friend: Written to Mrs. Ezra S. Carr, 1866-1879,* ed. William Frederic Badè (Boston: Houghton Mifflin, 1915; reprint ed., Dunwoody, Georgia: Norman S. Berg, 1973), pp. 48-52.

———————————

Throughout the spring months Muir thought about Yosemite and about visiting it once more. His opportunity came in June when he was invited to join a shepherd and his flock on their way to Tuolumne Meadows, in the northern extremes of Yosemite. It was precisely the area Muir wished to see. He quit the foothills and began this, his second trip to Yosemite. Years later when preparing his autobiography he used the journals of this trip as the basis for *My First Summer in the Sierra* (1911). We present here portions of those journals, exactly as they were written in 1869. Muir is here establishing his central theme: that experience, especially in the wilderness, is the only true wealth.

Also given is a letter written to his sister Ann—a revealing note, written at the end of the summer after Muir had completed his stay in the Sierra and was wondering what next to do. How much longer, he asks, can he remain a wanderer?

June 6. [1869]

Now we are fairly into the mountains, and they are into us. We are fairly living now. What bright seething white-fire enthusiasm is bred in us—without our help or knowledge. A perfect influx into every pore and cell of us, fusing, vaporizing by its heat until the boundary walls of our heavy flesh tabernacle seem taken down and we flow and diffuse into the very air and trees and streams and rocks, thrilling with them to the touch of the vital sunbeams. Responsive, we are part of nature now, neither old or young, but immortal in a terrestrial way, neither sick or well. I cannot now conceive of any bodily condition variable and dependent on food or breath any more than the granite stones or the sky. So dependent. How glorious a conversion, so complete and wholesome is it, scarce memory of old bondage days is left as a standpoint to view it from, even in the silence and darkness of the camp at night. We rather seem to have been so always. Nature like a fluid seems to drench and steep us throughout, as the whole sky and the rocks and flowers are drenched with spiritual life—with God. Now I am no longer a shepherd with a few bruised beans and crackers in my stomach and wrapped in a woolen blanket, but a free bit everything, not to be defined as to extent nor cramped or bound as to movements more than clouds are.

What a glorious drift I enjoyed when looking through the yellow pines today. I caught sight of the snowy peaks grouped about the headwaters of the Merced. How near they seemed and how clear their outlines on the blue air, or rather in the blue air, for they seemed saturated with the very substance of the sky. What promise they held out, and invitation, and how grand the attraction I felt. I would reach these sometime, I felt, and I would go to these in very love to learn whatever I might be able. Then it would all seem too good to be true. I would never be allowed so noble a duty—someone worthy would go and be blest. Yet will I drift about these mountains, movements of Divine love, near or far, here or there, willing—dearly loving to be but a servant of servants in this holy wilderness.

June 23. Oh, these glorious old mountain days, ripe and sweet and luscious like fruit to be eaten, yet better than ever fabled in the Garden of the Hesperdes. So hearty in their greeting, so warm and real yet so purely fine. So rocky and substantial yet so infinitely spiritual, exciting at once to work and rest, bestowing substance in its grandest forms. Yet throwing open a thousand windows to show us heaven. Never more shall man be weary or faint by the way who gains but the blessings of one mountain day. Whatever his fortune, he is rich forevermore.

Muir Papers, File 19.1, Sierra Journal, Summer of 1869, 1:28–29, 103.

July 11. [1869]

We are now about 7000 feet above the sea and the nights are cool and we have to pile coats and extra clothing on top of our blankets. The water in the Tamarac Creek is icy cold, hurts our teeth in drinking, delicious, exhilarating champagne water. It flows bank-full with silent speed through the long grass, but a few hundred yards below our camp the ground is bare gray granite strewn with enormous bowlders, large spaces without a single tree or only a small one here and there anchored in narrow seams and cracks. The bowlders are not in piles, scattered like rubbish among loose and crumbling debris as if weathered out of the solid as bowlders of disintegration, but they mostly occur singly, and are lying on a clean plantless pavement on which the sunshine is beating free, making a glare that contrasts most strikingly with the shimmer of light and shade we have been accustomed to in the leafy woods. And strange to say these huge bowlders, lying so still and deserted with no moving force near them, no bowlder carrier anywhere in sight, were never-the-less brought from a distance, quarried and carried and laid down here each in its place out on the bald granite pavement, under the stars, nor have they stirred through calm and storm since first they were laid here. They look lonely, strangers in a strange land—huge blocks mostly angular, mountain chips, 20 to 30 feet in diameter, some of them, the chips that Nature had made in modeling her landscapes. And what was the tool that quarried them and carried them. Looking on the pavement we soon find its marks. On the most resisting unweathered portions the surface is scored and striated in a rigidly parallel way indicating in the most unmistakable terms that the region has been over-swept by a great glacier from the northeastward, grinding down the mountains and giving them a strange raw wiped appearance, scoring and polishing the surface and leaving whatever bowlders it chanced to be carrying at the time it was melted at the close of the Glacial Period. A fine discovery this. As for the forests we have been passing through, they are mostly growing on deposits of soil laid down by the same ice-agent in the forms of moraines of different sorts.

Out of the grassy meadow and down through this bare granite-region, scored by glaciers, the happy young creek goes, bursting into a perfect bloom of falls and cascades, and singing and booming solemnly as a mighty river on its way to the bottom of the main cañon of the Merced, below the Yosemite

Valley, making a descent of more than 3000 feet in a distance of
about 2 miles.

All the Merced streams are wonderful singers and the
Yosemite Valley is the grand centre where the main tributarys
meet. I can see into the lower end of the Valley from a point half
a mile from camp. A grand page spread here and I would gladly
give my life to be able to read it. How vast it seems and
hopelessly deep and difficult, and life is so short, and our powers
so shallow. Yet why should one bewail one's poor feeble
ignorance. The beauty is visible and that we can enjoy, though
the grand mechanical causes may lie beyond our ken. Sing on
brave Tamarac Creek fresh from forest meadows, bounce and
dance and go down to your fate; go die in the seas, bathe the
ferns as you go, refresh the flowers and every living thing along
your banks as you go, a good way to waste yourself, from
beauty to beauty, passing unhalting, fruitful, as a star.

Muir Papers, File 19.2, Sierra Journal, Summer of 1869, 2:21–23.

Hopeton, Aug 15, '68 [1869]*

Dear twin Ann,

I was sorry to know that you had borrowed trouble over me,
your anxiety was of far too rapid a growth, having sprouted,
leafed, and fruited ere it had any business to come out of the
ground.

Those three months in which I was reported missing were the
floweriest of all the months of my existence; no matter what
direction I travelled I still waded in flowers by day, and slept
with them by night, hundreds of flowery gems of most surpassing loveliness touched my feet at every step, and buried them
out of sight. I was very happy, the larks and insects sang streams
of unmeasured joy, glorious mountain walls around me,—a sky
of plants beneath, and a sky of light above, all kept by their
Maker in perfect beauty and pure as heaven.

I am always a little lonesome, Annie. Ought I not to be a man
by this time and put away childish things? I have wandered far
enough, and seen strange faces enough to feel the whole world a

* The date given is somewhat of a mystery. Perhaps Muir misdated the
original letter, or perhaps Badè misdated during transcription. Almost certainly
the events described in this letter took place during the summer of 1869.

home, and I am a batchelor too. I should not be a boy, but I cannot accustom myself to the coldness of strangers, nor to the shiftings and wanderings of this Arab life.

Annie, I have not learned to know your handwriting yet, nor Mary's, nor Joanna's*—they are so constantly changing. You use the pen better than formerly, but there is still room for improvement. I do not like this pinched printed style, with heavy pendulum-bob markings upon the ts, ds, and ys. It is the painful, puckered, pictured system of the very exact maidens bred in the far west,—I hope you will endeavor to acquire a more sloping flowery [rest of the letter lost].

Muir Papers, Correspondence, Box 14, Letters Sent, 1860–1873.

The last items are jottings Muir made in later years, probably in the late 1870s. The older Muir here subsumes and reflects upon the experience of emergent Muir.

[Undated]

Friends are not left by walking a yard or a mile or 1000 miles from them. Arithmetic and geography have nothing to do with friendship, kindship. Miles and mountains, continents and seas play but a subordinate part in love affairs. Oftentimes we are nearest our friends when farthest from them. To true lovers it matters but little whether seas, mountains, or even death lie between them, there is yet no separation. Nothing loved can be left or lost sight of.

The wilderness is rather frugal in food for body but prodigal in its ministry to the mind. Not mere amusement but work—a collection of curious pictures and odd surprises for jaded forespent pleasure-seekers, but noble uplifing exhilarating work which we must do.

More wild knowledge, less arithmetic and grammar—compulsory education in the form of woodcraft, mountain craft, science at first hand.

Muir Papers, File 37.14, Autobiography, fragments.

* Muir's sisters.

Part Two

Among the Folds and Mazes of Yosemite's Falls (1869–1871)

I like to walk, touch living Mother Earth—bare feet best, and thrill every step. Used to envy happy reptiles that had advantage of so much body in contact with earth, bosom to bosom. [We] live with our heels as well as head and most of our pleasure comes in that way.

John Muir, Muir Papers, undated

At the summer's end, 1869, Muir quietly postponed plans to continue wandering and resolved to spend the winter in Yosemite Valley. Perhaps he felt a need to drop out of sight for awhile, isolate himself so that he might collect his thoughts and plan his future, while all along giving himself the chance to soak up the beauty of a region he felt more and more to be a home. He feared his family might consider this planned move silly and imprudent—or so he wrote his brother David— yet he was "bewitched" and "must go."* He arrived in the valley in November 1869 and hired on with pioneer James Hutchings as a handyman and sawyer. We give here Muir's account of the trip and of his impressions of Yosemite, as they appear in one of his first journals.

Yosemite. December, 1869

I left the foothills at French Bar November 16, 1869, with H. Randall, for Yosemite in particular, and the Sierra in general. We advanced slowly by unforced marches, making every principal mountain bench which we encountered the labor of a day— generally eating breakfast at the foot, dinner half-way up, and supper at the summit. We were armed with a very formidable stabbing instrument, a kind of halfway thing betwixt a sword and a butcher knife. At Coulterville we further armed and burdened ourselves with a shotgun and projectiles suited to the killing of all kinds of mountain life. The scenery was enchanting, and we allowed our bodies ample time to sponge it up. We found no snow, and in many places, upon sunny stream-banks, some late flowers were lingering like flies after frost. The magnificent conifer and King of Pines *Pinus lambertiana* warmed us with its beauty all the way from Coulterville. The lovely fir *Abies magnifica* towered in exact and measured grandeur in its unchangeable green. Maples and black oaks were casting their brown and yello leaves, and in their crumpling and rustling beneath our feet touched many a memory of the sweet Indian-summer days of the old West.

Linnie Marsh Wolfe, ed., *John of the Mountains: The Unpublished Journals of John Muir* (Boston: Houghton Mifflin, 1938; reprint ed., Madison: University of Wisconsin Press, 1979), p. 36.

---

* Letter to David Gilrye Muir, quoted in Linnie Marsh Wolfe, *Son of the Wilderness: The Life of John Muir* (New York: Knopf, 1945; reprint ed., Madison: University of Wisconsin Press, 1978) p. 124.

Sketch of John Muir's cabin at the base of Yosemite Falls. John Muir Papers, Holt-Atherton Department of Special Collections, University of the Pacific Libraries. Copyright 1984 Muir-Hanna Trust.

Soon Muir had constructed a sawmill and a small cabin, along Yosemite Creek beneath the great falls. Here he worked and lived with his friend, and from the cabin wrote to his brother David: "I am sitting here in a little shanty made of sugarpine shingles this Sabbath evening. I have not been at church a single time since leaving home. Yet this glorious valley might well be called a church, for every lover of the great Creator who comes within the broad overwhelming influences of the place fails not to worship as they never did before."*

Muir was to spend the next year and a half working in the mill and in guiding tourists around the valley. The prominent and the not-so-famous were to meet him, some sent by Mrs. Carr, others attracted by the odd, ecstatic statements of the man at the sawmill. Muir's inner struggle to settle and please his family faded by degrees during these months, as the restlessness to travel was transformed into a need to explore the walls and recesses of Yosemite. Little escaped his attention—as the following journal entries suggest.

January 18 [1870]

If my soul could get away from this so-called prison, be granted all the list of attributes generally bestowed on spirits, my first ramble on spirit wings would not be among the volcanoes of the moon. Nor should I follow the sunbeams to their sources in the sun. I should hover about the beauty of our own good star. I should not go moping among the tombs, nor around the artificial desolation of men. I should study Nature's laws in all their crossings and unions; I should follow magnetic streams to their source, and follow the shores of our magnetic oceans. I should go among the rays of the aurora, and follow them to their beginnings, and study their dealings and communions with other powers and expressions of matter. And I should go to the very center of our globe and read the whole splendid page from the beginning.

But my first journeys would be into the inner substance of flowers, and among the folds and mazes of Yosemite's falls. How grand to move about in the very tissue of falling columns, and in the very birthplace of their heavenly harmonies, looking outward as from windows of ever-varying transparency and straining!

Alas, how little of the world is subject to human senses!

* Letter to David Gilrye Muir, March 20, 1870, quoted in William Frederic Badè, *The Life and Letters of John Muir*, 2 vols. (Boston: Houghton Mifflin, 1923–24), 1:209.

March 25

Birds, bats, and butterflies in fervent motion. Cloud on Tissiack. Snow-slides from Dome like falls. Waterfalls striking louder notes. Spring!

May 5

These beautiful days must enrich all my life. They do not exist as mere pictures—maps hung upon the walls of memory to brighten at times when touched by association or will, only to sink again like a landscape in the dark; but they saturate themselves unto every part of the body and live always.

May 23

Warmer and the river is rising. The falls are at the stage of greatest palpable display.

May 25

Warm, genial days of transition from spring to summer. Magnificent groups of cumuli rise almost daily from the summits at eleven o'clock A.M., making a rich background for the fringing trees of the valley rim.

Wolfe, ed., *John of the Mountains*, pp. 43–44, 47, 53.

———————

Muir kept up his correspondence during these months, and told Mrs. Carr about his new-found sense of freedom, his joy in watching the Yosemite's changing moods—and his disdain for the tourists who visited the valley but did not, in his view, pause to worship or to understand it:

Yosemite, July *29th* [1870]

I am very, very blessed. The Valley is full of people, but they do not annoy me. I revolve in pathless places and in higher rocks than *the world* and his ribbony wife can reach. Had I not been blunted by hard work in the mill, and crazed by Sabbath raids among the high places of this heaven, I would have written you long since. I have spent every Sabbath for the last two months in the spirit world, screaming among the peaks and outside meadows like a negro Methodist in revival time, and every intervening clump of week days in trying to fix down and assimilate my shapeless harvests of revealed glory into the spirit and into the common earth of my existence, and I am rich—rich beyond measure, not in rectangular blocks of sifted knowledge, or in thin sheets of beauty hung picture-like about the "walls of memory," but in unselected atmospheres of terrestrial glory diffused evenly throughout my whole substance. . . .

William Frederic Badè, *The Life and Letters of John Muir,* 2 vols. (Boston: Houghton Mifflin, 1923–24), 1:226.

To his brother Daniel he gave a further description of his keen and prolonged contact with the wilderness, and then, showing practical mood, promises to help finance his brother's medical training.

Yosemite, June 4, 1871.

Dear brother

Some time ago I rec'd a letter from you in which you requested a loan of a few dollars etc. I answered at once saying that I would willingly send you what you wanted if I could get out of the valley in the fall to send it. I addressed the letter to Ann Arbor & perhaps you have not rec'd it. As long as I have a dollar you are far more than welcome to it if you need it & I hope that you will not allow yourself to suffer for anything that you require. I am in the heart of the mtns or I would send you $200 at once.

I am glad to hear that you have opened an office & now let me say to you, be cheerful & hopeful. The best of physicians generally have a slow recognition of their talents & may have to go through a sort of starving period before they are known & appreciated, but be stout of heart, you have many friends & will even have more & I suppose a true woman to share your joys & trials & labors. & Brother at this distance I reach my hand to you & press it with all the warmth of confiding affection & say that you shall never know a want that I can relieve wherever I may roam.

Remember me very kindly to your love & say that I will be very happy to know her.

I am working hard in every way but enjoy most of the work.
Sometimes operating the sawmill, sometimes guiding in the
mtns. I am more & more interested in science & am making
many friends among the learned & the good who all seem to hail
me as a brother.

I have no fixed practical aim, but am living in constant communion with Nature & follow my instincts & am most intensely
happy.

Some day you will also behold the Lord's Yosemite.

I went to a noted point at the top of the Valley wall today &
am a little footsore. Yesterday I went alone up the rocks to the
upper Yosemite Fall & back in the night (a day's work) after
doing my day's work to enjoy the glory of the fall in the
moonlight. Not long ago I was at the summit of the Mt. Hoffman with an English man & a Scotch man.

Farewell

Be hopeful & patient & do not overwork yourself. I have full
confidence in you & am your brother.

Elizabeth I. Dixon, ed., "Some New John Muir Letters," *Southern California Quarterly* 46,
no. 3 (September 1964): 249–50.

Muir's fear that his life might be aimless eventually faded away. He
summed up his thoughts about his career during this spring and
summer of 1871 in notes which seem to be written about this time but
whose date cannot be pinned down. He would let go of the old bondage
days (his term) and enter freely into the study of Yosemite's glaciers and
Yosemite's beauty. Like a sponge he would soak up whatever lessons he
might meet regardless of their apparent value—regardless whether
society might understand his motives or conduct. He would be, he
writes, "wholly free—born again!"

[Undated]

There are eight members in our family. All are useful members
of society—save me. One is a healer of the sick. Another a
merchant, and a deacon in good standing. The rest school
teachers and farmers' wives—all exemplary, stable, anti-
revolutionary. Surely, then, thought I, one may be spared for so
fine an experiment. The remnants of compunction—the struggle

concerning that serious business of settling down—gradually wasted and melted, and at length left me wholly free—born again!

I will follow my instincts, be myself for good or ill, and see what will be the upshot. As long as I live, I'll hear waterfalls and birds and winds sing. I'll interpret the rocks, learn the language of flood, storm, and the avalanche. I'll acquaint myself with the glaciers and wild gardens, and get as near the heart of the world as I can.

Hunger and cold, getting a living, hard work, poverty, loneliness, need of renumeration, giving up all thought of being known, getting married, etc., made no difference.

From Linnie Marsh Wolfe, *Son of the Wilderness: The Life of John Muir* (New York: Knopf, 1945; reprint ed., Madison: University of Wisconsin Press, 1978), p. 144.

The summer of 1871 was a period of transition in the life and intent of John Muir. While in June he told his brother Daniel he had "no fixed practical aim," by the fall he believed his life's work was plainly evident. He wrote his mother that he understood how the Yosemite Valley and all the mountains of the Sierra had been formed, and that he was going to study their creation, and perhaps even write a book.

The proof of the glacial origin of Yosemite came to Muir one Sunday in July 1871 when he realized that the Yosemite Creek Basin, on the north rim of the valley, was itself the result of glacial erosion. The hypothesis would also, Muir knew, explain the creation of all the Yosemite's canyons, even of the great valley of the Merced. He described how the theory came to him in a letter he wrote to Ralph Waldo Emerson soon after the pair had spent their memorable week together in the valley and among the Mariposa Big Trees. (The "Samoset" mentioned in the letter refers to a tree named by Emerson. See also the Thayer account, in Part III, below.)

Yosemite, July 6th [1871]

Dear Emerson,

You are in the calm of home & perhaps will be glad to hear this small echo from our Mariposa trees. Here is Samoset with whom you are acquainted & with whom I spent a night & day. He is noble in form & behavior as any Sequoia friend that I have—less proper—less orthodox than his two companions but has more dignity—more freedom, wh'[ich] he manifests by the curving and thrusting of every limb.

All three touch & intermingle at the top—at least when breathed upon by the winds.

Some spirey, arrowy firs'are poised about his brown trunk which makes a magnificent background for their level benches of silvery spray. Among his other friends living far below in his shadow are the Ceanothus & the rose & the lupine & violet & the broad shouldered bracken.

And little mosses and lichens also—humblest children of the Kingdom, meet King Sequoia & dwell with him & they paint his grand column with their green & gold as big congregations of social flowers color the flutings of the hillside.

I remember some of your party remarked the silence of our woods & the absence of birds. Well, ere you were half way down the hill a gush of the richest forest song that ever tingled human soul came in grand confidence from the whole grove choir of trees, birds & flies. When you went away I walked to the top of the ridge commanding a view of the arterial groves of the Fresnoe, to calm, & when I returned to the grove near Samoset I was welcomed by five or six birds. The magnificent pileated woodpecker eighteen inches in length came right up to me & turned round & round as if anxious that I should know all his gestures & notes & observe the color & polish of every feather. A little brown specky titmouse was building a house near the ground beneath a flake of Sequoia bark & she allowed me to remain within five feet of her building without ceasing her work, only pausing an instant now & then to look at me. Also a very shy slim ashcovered bird about the size of the robin shewed himself occasionally. He is swift & impulsive in flight & frequently hovers about the ends of spruce boughs like a humming bird. A lot of chickadee like birds flitted about like moths & one with a rich flutey voice approached in the Ceanothus tangle but did not show himself & after all these were sleeping a big-voiced owl echoed the solemn grove from end to end, & next day as I drifted slowly down to the lower trees I saw birds everywhere: —the Grizzly Giant was full of birds, & as I was about to start for Clarks while I lingered among the farewell impressions at the base of the last Sequoia a bird came down to one of the lowest branches near my head &

uttered loud & clear a bosomful of the most startling wooded song that I ever felt. From first to last all of Nature seemed to hear the call of another King David & joined in one grand rejoicing. There was the sweetest wavings & hushings of trees hummings of insect wings—open jointed warblings of birds & the rocks too pulsed to the general joy, & every crystal and individual dust—

In a few days I start for the high Sierra East of Yosemite & I would willingly walk all the way to your Concord if so I could have you for a companion—the indians & hot plains would be nothing. In particular I want to study a certain pine-tree at different elevations, & the lavas of Mono.

The dear Mother has told me of one magnificent truth since you were last here. Two years ago I crossed the basin of Yosemite Creek a mile or two back of the top of the falls & observed what appeared as indications of a glacier, & again about a month ago I was upon Mt Hoffman & on my return to the Valley crossed the Yosemite basin & received still more satisfactory hints of the former existence of a glacier wh' flowed at right angles to those later & larger ones of the summits.

Now there is a very deep cañon on the left of Yosemite falls wh' has compelled me to think to it every day for more than a year & I could not account for its formation in any other way than by supposing the existence of a glacier in the basin above as one of the conditions. Last Sabbath the big truth came to the birth. I ran out of the Valley by Indian Cañon, & round to the top of the falls—said my prayers in the irised spray & started for the upper end of the basin ten or twelve miles distant hoping somewhere to discover positive evidence of my missing glacier in the higher deeper portions of its channel where it would linger longest or where it had been compelled to wedge through some narrow place thus hardening & more deeply groving the granite wh' then would not be so susceptible of disintegration.

Well I had not gone four miles ere I found all I had so long sought & you might have heard a shout in Concord.

This glacier was about 12 m's [miles] in length by about 6 in breadth.* Of the depth I have as yet no data. Its course was

---

* Muir is here referring to the length and breadth of an ancient glacier which had once occupied the basin.

nearly at right angles to the summit glaciers & perhaps it was not born quite so early as they. & I am sure that it died long before they were driven from the cañons of the Tenaya & Nevada streams. I have just finished a first reading of your Society & Solitude. The poems I have read several times. I have been very deeply interested with them am far from being done with them. Excepting the woodnotes wh' M$^{rs.}$ Carr read me & the Burley bumblebee I have not seen any of your poems before.

Since I cannot have yourself I want your photograph.

Ever Yours,

JOHN MUIR

Ralph L. Rusk, ed., *The Letters of Ralph Waldo Emerson,* 6 vols. (New York: Columbia University Press, 1939), 6:155–57.

In the following long and important letter, Muir tells of his discoveries, personal as well as geological. He tells Mrs. Carr that he is involved with the study of glaciers and with reading the Sierra's alphabet of rock and ice; he might even produce a manuscript and send it to the Boston Academy of Science. He asks Carr's opinion on how he might go about publishing some of the thoughts written in his journals. Clearly the intent now is to understand the Yosemite and then to explain it to the public. He will continue searching for the key to Yosemite's creation, he writes, for he has no choice but to pursue the "glorious results" of his studies.

Yosemite, September 8th, 1871

Dear Friend:

I am sorry King* made you uneasy about me. He does not understand me as you do, and you must not heed him so much. He thinks that I am melancholy, and above all that I require polishing. I feel sure that if you were here to see how happy I am, and how ardently I am seeking a knowledge of the rocks you could not call me away, but would gladly let me go only with God and his written rocks to guide me. You would not think of calling me to make machines or a home, or of setting me up for measurement. No, dear friend, you would say, "Keep your mind untrammeled and pure. Go unfrictioned, unmeasured, and God give you the true meaning and interpretation of his mountains."

You know that for the last three years I have been ploddingly

---

* Not the mountaineer-geologist Clarence King.

making observations about this Valley and the high mountains to the East of it, drifting broodingly about and taking in every natural lesson that I was fitted to absorb. In particular the great Valley has always kept a place in my mind. How did the Lord make it? What tools did He use? How did He apply them and when? I considered the sky above it and all of the opening cañons, and studied the forces that came in by every door that I saw standing open, but I could get no light. Then I said, "You are attempting what is not possible for you to accomplish. Yosemite is the *end* of a grand chapter. If you would learn to read it go commence at the beginning." Then I went above to the alphabet valleys of the summits, comparing cañon with cañon, with all their varieties of rock structure and cleavage, and comparative size and slope of the glaciers and waters which they contained. Also the grand congregation of rock creations were present to me, and I studied their forms and sculpture. I soon had a key to every Yosemite rock and perpendicular and sloping wall. The grandeur of these forces and their glorious results overpower me, and inhabit my whole being. Waking or sleeping I have no rest. In dreams I read blurred sheets of glacial writing or follow lines of cleavage or struggle with the difficulties of some extraordinary rock form. Now it is clear that woe is me if I do not drown this tendency toward nervous prostration by constant labor in working up the details of this whole question. I have been down from the upper rocks only three days and am hungry for exercise already.

Professor Runkle,* President of the Massachusetts Institute of Technology, was here last week, and I preached my glacial theory to him for five days, taking him into the cañons of the Valley and up among the grand glacier wombs and pathways of the summit. He was fully convinced of the truth of my readings, and urged me to write out the glacial system of Yosemite and its tributaries for the Boston Academy of Science. I told him I meant to write my thoughts for my own use and that I would send him the manuscript and if he and his wise scientific brothers thought it of sufficient interest they might publish it.

---

* John Daniel Runkle.

He is going to send me some instruments, and I mean to go over all the glacier basins carefully, working until driven down by the snow. In winter I can make my drawings and maps and write out notes. So you see that for a year or two I will be very busy.

I have settled with Hutchings and have no dealings with him now.* I think that next spring I will have to guide a month or two for pocket money, although I do not like the work. I suppose I might live for one or two seasons without work. I have five hundred dollars here, and I have been sending home money to my sisters and brothers—perhaps about twelve or fifteen hundred, and a man in Canada owes me three or four hundred dollars more which I suppose I could get if I was in need; but you know that the Scotch do not like to spend their last dollar. Some of my friends are badgering me to write for some of the magazines, and I am almost tempted to try it, only I am afraid that this would distract my mind from my main work more than the distasteful and depressing labor of the mill or of guiding. What do you think about it?

Suppose I should give you some of the journals my [sic] first thoughts about this glacier work as I go along and afterwards gather them and press them for the Boston wise; or will it be better to hold my *wheesht*† and say it all at a breath? You see how practical I have become, and how fully I have burdened you with my little affairs!

Perhaps you will ask, "What plan are you going to pursue in your work?" Well, here it is—the only book I ever invented. First, I will describe each glacier with its tributaries separately, then describe the rocks and hills and mountains *over* which they have flowed or *past* which they have flowed, endeavoring to prove that all of the various forms which those rocks now have is the necessary result of the ice action in connection with their structure and cleavage, etc.—also the different kinds of cañons and lake basins and meadows which they have made. Then, armed with these data, I will come down to Yosemite, where all

* Hutching's quarrel was over the time Muir was spending away from the sawmill.

† Scotch word for "silence."

of my ice has come, and prove that each dome and brow and wall, and every face and spire and brother is the necessary result of the delicately balanced blows of well directed and combined glaciers against the parent rocks which contained them, only thinly carved and moulded in some instances by the subsequent action of water, etc.

Libby sent me Tyndall's* new book, and I have looked hastily over it. It is an alpine mixture of very pleasant taste, and I wish I could enjoy reading and talking it with you. I expect Mrs. Hutchings will accompany her husband to the East this winter, and there will not be one left with whom I can exchange a thought. Mrs. Hutchings is going to leave me all the books I want, and Runkle is going to send me Darwin. These, with my notes and maps, will fill my winter hours, if my eyes do not fail. And now that you see my whole position I think that you would not call me to the excitements and distracting novelties of civilization.

This bread question is very troublesome. I will eat anything you think will suit me. Send up either by express to Big Oak Flat or by any other chance, and I will remit the money required in any way you like.

My love to all and more thanks than I can write for your constant kindness.

Badè, *Life and Letters*, 1:293–98.

––––––––––––

Muir completed his break with Wisconsin during the fall of 1871. Convinced that he must go his own way, he asks his brother Daniel to send to Yosemite whatever small possessions remain at Indianapolis. He also confides that he will not soon be marrying, perhaps not until he is "too old," as he is now convinced nothing should hinder his studies of the Yosemite.

Yosemite
Nov. 1st, 1871

Dear Brother Medicus,

I am glad to hear of your successes & comforts present, past, & prospective, but am very sorry that you so much need money

* John Tyndall, geologist and alpinist.

at a time that I cannot collect any for you. You might have had three or four hundred more if you had let me know sooner. I have written at least three letters to you ere I read this one relative to the hundred dollar note.

I think you are right about conjugating. I will now be spending money without making much, as I have commenced the work of making a book for the Boston Academy of Sciences on the Ancient Glacial Systems of the Merced, wh[ich] will occupy my time for several years. Still I will make a few dollars in summer & if you find yourself very needful next year let me know by June or July & I will save a little for you. I shall not need marrying money for some years, perhaps not until I am too old, so when I have any money you are welcome to it.

I have not heard from Miss Pelton for a long time but I believe she is somewhere in the northern portion of this state. *

Give my compliments to your love whom I have not yet seen but whom I am sure to like if she is at all worthy of you.

I will be much obliged to you for packing & shipping my Indianapolis trunk. You alone are able to handle my models etc. Pack my trunk with my thermometer (this one) & scythe clock which I will need in my cabin & wh[ich] will cost but little for freight. Also such tools as are *light* & easily packed & with such of my clothes as are worth sending. I left at least one suit of good clothes. My three or four fine shirts keep & wear, as they would be of no use to me, also anything else wh[ich] you need or want.

Send also my scientific & blank books & dictionary. I do not want the doctor book wh[ich] you will find in my trunk, nor any of my school books. Of pictures send me Red Jacket & Fountain Lake & *Home* & the drawing on my desk.

My plants give in charge to Mrs. Moores if she has room for them, if not box & send to Sarah.†

You will find Mrs. Moores at 145 Merrill St. Of my few other goods & chattels, take what will in any way serve yourself & box and send all the rest to Sarah care of D[avid] G. Muir, Portage [Wisconsin]. Do not pay the expressage on anything &

* Emily Pelton moved in 1871 to the Marysville region, north of Sacramento, where she was to live for many years.

† The Moores were friends of Muir. Sarah is Muir's sister.

what expense you are at debt to me or draw on Dave—I do not expect that Mr. Sutherland will charge anything for storage as they told me when I left that they would not be in the way & agreed to keep them for me. Mrs. S. has the key to my trunk.

JOHN MUIR
Yosemite Valley
California
(Via Coulterville)

I hope that you will never allow yourself to be pinched for money again if I can get any for you. Farewell, I cannot come to you: I am bound to the mountains but anear or afar am ever yours in family love.

I sleep out weeks alone in the upper mtns among the bears but they manifest no disposition to touch me. We will someday drink champagne over those nights wh[ich] we passed in the company of Canada wolves.

Elizabeth I. Dixon, ed., "Some New John Muir Letters," pp. 250–51.

Muir was by degrees coming to believe that his so-called aimless wanderings might eventually lead to some publishable writings, although he was not yet sure of their precise form or content; nonetheless he wrote to his mother at this time that he was hard at work ("God's work," he calls it) and was convinced he was being guided to the truth. Soon, he tells her, he will be collecting his discoveries into some sort of "human book."

With its sharply defined metaphor and vibrant rhythms, what follows is doubtless among the finest letters written during Muir's time in Yosemite.

Yosemite Valley
November 16th, [1871]

Dear Mother,

Our highwalled home is quiet now; travel has ceased for the season, and I have returned from my last hard exploratory ramble in the summit mountains. I will remain during the winter at Black's Hotel, taking care of the premises and working up the data which I have garnered during these last months and years concerning the ancient glacial system of this wonderful region.

For the last two or three months I have worked incessantly among the most remote and undiscoverable of the deep cañons of this pierced basin, finding many a mountain page glorious with the writing of God and in characters that any earnest eye could read. The few scientific men who have written upon this region tell us that Yosemite Valley is unlike anything else, an exceptional creation, separate in all respects from all other valleys, but such is not true. Yosemite is one of *many,* one chapter of a great mountain book written by the same pen of ice which the Lord long ago passed over every page of our great Sierra Nevadas. I know how Yosemite and all the other valleys of these magnificent mountains were made and the next year or two of my life will be occupied chiefly in writing their history in a human book—a glorious subject, which God help me preach aright.

I have been sleeping in the rocks and snow, often weary and hungry, sustained by the excitements of my subject and by the Scottish pluck and perseverance which belongs to our family. For the last few days I have been eating and resting and enjoying long warm sleeps beneath a roof, in a warm, rockless, boulderless bed.

In all my lonely journeys among the most distant and difficult pathless, passless mountains, I never wander, am never lost. Providence guides through every danger and takes me to all the truths which I need to learn, and some day I hope to show you my sheaves, my big bound pages of mountain gospel.

I have been busy moving my few chattels from Hutchings' to Black's, about half a mile down the Valley, and I scarce feel at home. Tidings of the great far sweeping fires have reached our hidden home, and I am thankful that your section of towns and farms have been spared. I heard a few weeks ago from David and Joanna and learned all is well. Wisconsin winter will soon be upon you. May you enjoy its brightness and universal beauty in warm and happy homes.

Out topmost mountains are white with their earliest snow, but the Valley is still bare and brown with rustling leaves of the oak and alder and fronds of the fast fading ferns. Between two and three thousand persons visited the Valley this summer. I am glad they are all gone. I can now think my thoughts and say my prayers in quiet.

Ever devoutly yours in family love.

JOHN MUIR

Badè, *Life and Letters*, 1:314–16.

The article which had been forming in Muir's mind finally took shape and he submitted it to Horace Greeley's *New York Tribune*. Taking phrases and sometimes whole passages from letters to friends (including the one to Emerson), Muir presented his article to the public. To his delight, and perhaps surprise, it was purchased for two hundred dollars, a handsome sum in his day, and was read by the leading naturalists of the East. It was his first published piece, and although "Yosemite Glaciers: The Ice Streams of the Great Valley," was listed anonymously, as a contribution "from an occasional correspondent," Muir's friends and scientific acquaintances in Boston knew it was his work.*

This article was a significant contribution to the study of glaciology. It also marked the beginning of the controversy between Muir and Josiah Whitney, State Geologist of California, who had already published his view that Yosemite was the creation of some great prehistoric cataclysmic fall. The debate, amply recorded in biographies of Muir, was to finally subside, but not before Whitney's staff member Clarence King was to call Muir an "ambitious amateur" whose theories led only to "hopeless floundering."†

The theories which Muir presents in the article are not wholly correct. Muir believed in Louis Agassiz's hypothesis that there had been one Ice Age which had swept over all the northern continents; Muir believed the Sierra glaciers were remnants of this ice sheet and that the canyons had been carved out almost solely by their force. In fact, there were at least four distinct ice-epochs, and the "living glaciers" which Muir was finding in the Sierra were actually distinct and independent glaciers, formed by the moist, cool air entering the region through the Golden Gate. Nonetheless, Muir was correct to think conditions in the

---

* This *Tribune* article is doubtless Muir's first manuscript to be published. Muir himself once listed an article, "Calypso," dated 1864 or 1865, and appearing in the *Boston Recorder,* as his first published article; however, a careful search by the editors and by the staff of the Boston Congregational Library failed to turn up "Calypso," or any article or letter ascribed to John Muir.

† Josiah Whitney's views are expressed in his *Yosemite Guide-Book* (Cambridge, Mass.: University Press, 1869). Clarence King's criticism of Muir is in King, ed., *Systematic Geology: Report of the Fortieth Parallel Survey* (Washington, D.C.: U.S. Government Printing Office, 1878), p. 478.

Sierra had made glaciers possible, and he was right in guessing that ice had been the primary agent in the creation of Yosemite Valley.*

Muir's glacial hypothesis exploded Whitney's catastrophe theory once for all. Yet even without evidence, Muir would not have accepted that a rift could have appeared in Nature's plenitude: "When we try to pick out anything by itself," he once said, "we find it hitched to everything else in the universe." Nature was a principle of unity, then, and by implication a critique of the industrialized society, with its fragmentation of the self, from which Muir had only recently fled. At this critical moment of encroaching alienation, the genre of descriptive prose, begun by that other Calvinist Scot, Ruskin, whom Muir had read, developed as one literary attempt to imagine nineteenth-century society back into a sacred unity.

Muir's article is a remarkable performance. He manages the perfect exposition of a scientific theory, but gracefully and casually, and with a human voice which takes its human perspective into account. There is much here that is characteristic of Muir's later writing: the use of his journals as experiential data; the striking metaphors of book and temple and womb; the delicate anthropomorphizing of natural objects; basing the exposition on the narrative of Muir himself moving through a territory, at a walking pace. The tone and the very rhymes and rhythms of the last sentence here—"Good-night to my two logs and two lakes"—are the stylistic signatures of a man who is emerging as a writer.

Yosemite Glaciers

Yosemite Valley, Cal., Sept 28—Two years ago, when picking flowers in the mountains back of Yosemite Valley, I found a book. It was blotted and storm-beaten; all of its outer pages were mealy and crumbly, the paper seemed to dissolve like the snow beneath which it had been buried; but many of the inner pages were well preserved, and though all were more or less stained and torn, whole chapters were easily readable. In this condition is the great open book of Yosemite glaciers to-day; its granite pages have been torn and blurred by the same storms that wasted the castaway book. The grand central chapters of the Hoffman, and Tenaya, and Nevada glaciers are stained and corroded by the frosts and rains, yet, nevertheless, they contain scarce one unreadable page; but the outer chapters of the Pohono, and the Illilouette, and the Yosemite Creek, and Ribbon, and Cascade glaciers, are all dimmed and eaten away

* See François E. Matthes, *The Incomparable Valley: A Geologic Interpretation of the Yosemite* (Berkeley: University of California Press, 1950).

on the bottom, though the tops of their pages have not been so long exposed, and still proclaim in splendid characters the glorious actions of their departed ice. The glacier which filled the basin of the Yosemite Creek was the fourth ice-stream that flowed to Yosemite Valley. It was about fifteen miles in length by five in breadth at the middle of the main stream, and in many places was not less than 1,000 feet in depth. It united with the central glaciers in the valley by a mouth reaching from the east side of El Capitan to Yosemite Point, east of the falls. Its western rim was rayed with short tributaries, and on the north its divide from the Tuolumne glacier was deeply grooved; but few if any of its ridges were here high enough to separate the descending ice into distinct tributaries. The main central trunk flowed nearly south, and, at a distance of about 10 miles, separated into three nearly equal branches, which were turned abruptly to the east.

Branch Basins. Those branch basins are laid among the highest spurs of the Hoffman range, and abound in small, bright lakes, set in the solid granite without the usual terminal moraine dam. The structure of those dividing spurs is exactly similar, all three appearing as if ruins of one mountain, or rather as perfect units hewn from one mountain rock during long ages of glacial activity. As their north sides are precipitous, and as they extend east and west, they were enabled to shelter and keep alive their hiding glaciers long after the death of the main trunk. Their basins are still dazzling bright, and their lakes have as yet accumulated but narrow rings of border meadow, because their feeding streams have had but little time to carry the sand of which they are made. The east bank of the main stream, all the way from the three forks to the mouth, is a continuous, regular wall, which also forms the west bank of the Indian Canon glacier-basin. The tributaries of the west side of the main basin touched the east tributaries of the cascade, and the great Tuolumne glacier from Mount Dana, the mightiest ice-river of this whole region, flowed past on the north. The declivity of the tributaries was great, especially those which flowed from the spurs of the Hoffman on the Tuolumne divide, but the main stream was rather level, and in approaching Yosemite was compelled to make a considerable ascent back of Eagle Cliff. To the concentrated currents of the central glaciers, and to the levelness and width of mouth of this one, we in a great measure owe the present height of the Yosemite Falls. Yosemite Creek lives the most tranquil life of all the large streams that leap into the valley, the others occupying the cañons of narrower and, consequently, of deeper glaciers, while yet far from the valley, abound in loud falls and snowy cascades, but Yosemite Creek flows straight on through smooth meadows and hollows, with only two or three gentle cascades, and now and then a row of soothing, rumbling rapids, biding its time, and hoarding up the best music and poetry of its life for the one anthem at Yosemite, as planned by the ice.

Yosemite Basin. When a birdseye view of Yosemite Basin is obtained from any of its upper domes, it is seen to possess a great number of dense patches of black forest, planted in abrupt contact with bare gray rocks. Those forest plots mark the number and the size of all the entire and fragmentary moraines of the basin, as the latter eroding agents have not yet had sufficient time to form a soil fit for the vigorous life of large trees.

Wherever a deep-wombed tributary was laid against a narrow ridge, and was also shielded from the sun by compassing rock-shadows, there we invariably find on eor more small terminal moraines, because when such tributaries were melted off from the trunk they retired to those upper strongholds of shade, and lived and worked in full independence, and the moraines which they built are left entire because the water-collecting basins behind are too small to make streams large enough to wash them away; but in the basins of exposed tributaries there are no terminal moraines, because their glaciers died with the trunk. Medial and lateral moraines are common upon all the outside slopes, some of them nearly perfect in form; but down in the main basin there is not left one unaltered moraine of any kind, immense floods having washed down and leveled them into harder meadows for the present stream, and into sandy flower beds and fields for forests.

Glacier History. Such was Yosemite glacier, and such is its basin, the magnificent work of its hands. There is sublimity in the life of a glacier. Water rivers work openly, and so the rains and the gentle dews, and the great sea also grasping all the world: and even the universal ocean of breath, though invisible, yet speaks aloud in a thousand voices, and proclaims its modes of working and its power: but glaciers work apart from men, exerting their tremendous energies in silence and darkness, outspread, spirit-like, brooding above predestined rocks unknown to light, unborn, working on unwearied through unmeasured times, unhalting as the stars, until at length, their creations complete, their mountains brought forth, homes made for the meadows and the lakes, and fields for waiting forests, earnest, calm as when they came as crystals from the sky, they depart.

The great Valley itself, together with all its domes and walls, was brought forth and fashioned by a grand combination of glaciers, acting in certain directions against granite of peculiar physical structure. All of the rocks and mountains and lakes and meadows of the whole upper Merced basin received their specific forms and carvings almost entirely from this same agency of ice.

I have been drifting about among the rocks of this region for several years, anxious to spell out some of the mountain truths which are written here; and since the number, and magnitude, and significance of these ice-rivers began to appear, I have become anxious for more exact knowledge regarding them; with this object, supplying myself with blankets and bread, I climbed out of the Yosemite by Indian Cañon, and am now searching the upper rocks and moraines for readable glacier manuscript.

I meant to begin by exploring the main trunk glacier of Yo-semite Creek, together with all of its rim tributaries one by one, gathering what data I could find regarding their depth, direction of flow, the kind and amount of work which each had done, *etc.*, but when I was upon the El Capitan Mountain, seeking for the western shore of the main stream, I discovered that the Yosemite Creek glacier was not the lowest [most western] ice stream which flowed to the valley, but that the Ribbon Stream basin west of El Capitan had also been occupied by a glacier, which flowed nearly south, and united with the main central glaciers of the summits in the valley below El Capitan.

Ribbon Stream Basin. I spent two days in this new basin. It must have been one of the smallest ice streams that entered the valley, being only about four miles in length by three in width. It received some small tributaries from the slopes of El Capitan ridge, which flowed south 35° west; but most of the ice was derived from a spur of the Hoffman group, running nearly southwest. The slope of its bed is steep and pretty regular, and it must have flowed with considerable velocity. I have not thus far discovered any of the original striated surfaces, though possibly some patches may still exist somewhere in the basin upon hard plates of quartz, or where a bowlder of protecting form has settled upon a rounded surface. I found many such patches in the basin of Yosemite Glacier; some within a mile of the top of the falls—about two feet square in extent of surface, very perfect in polish, and its striae distinct, although the surrounding un-protected rock is disintegrated to a depth of at least four inches. As this small glacier sloped fully with unsheltered bosom to the sun, it was one of the first to die, and of course its tablets have been longer exposed to blurring rains and dews, and all eroding agents; but notwithstanding the countless blotting, crumbling storms which have fallen upon the historic lithographs of its surface, the great truth of its former existence printed in characters of moraine and meadow and valley groove, is still as clear as when every one of its pebbles and new-born rocks gleamed forth the full sun-shadowed poetry of its whole life. With the exception of a few castled piles and broken domes upon its east banks, its basin is rather smooth and lake-like, but it has charming meadows, most interesting in their present flora and glacier history, and noble forest of the two silver firs (Picea Amabilis and P. grandis)* planted upon moraines spread out and leveled by overflowing waters.

These researches in the basin of the Ribbon Creek recalled some observations made by me some time ago in the lower

---

* Silver firs do not grow in California. Muir is probably referring to the white fir (*Abies concolor*) and red fir (*Abies magnifica*).

portions of the basins of the Cascade and Tamarac streams, and I now thought it probable that careful search would discover abundant traces of glacial action in those basins also. Accordingly, on reaching the highest northern slope of the Ribbon, I obtained comprehensive views of both the Cascade and Tamarac basins, and amid their countless adornments could note many forms of lake and rock which appeared as genuine glacial characters unmarred and unaltered. Running down the bare slope of an icy-looking cañon, in less than half an hour I came upon a large patch of the old glacier bed, polished and striated, with the direction of the flow of the long dead glacier clearly written—South 40° West. This proved to be the lowest, eastern-most tributary of the Cascade glacier. I proceeded westward as far as the Cascade meadows on the Mons trail, then turning to the right, entered the mouth of the tributary at the head of the meadows. Here there is a well defined terminal moraine, and the ends of both ridges which formed the banks of the ice are broken and precipitous, giving evidence of great pressure. I followed up this tributary to its source on the west bank of the Yosemite glacier about two miles north of the Mono trail, and throughout its entire length there is abundance of polished tablets with moraines, rock scupture, *etc.,* giving glacier testimony as clear and indisputable as can be found in the most recent glacier pathways of the Alps.

Vanished Glaciers. I would gladly have explored the main trunk of this beautiful basin, from the highest snows upon the divide of the Tuolumne, to its mouth in the Merced Cañon below Yosemite, but alas! I had not sufficent bread, besides I felt sure that I should also have to explore the Tamarac basin, and, following westward among the fainter, most changed, and covered glacier pathways, I might probably be called as far as the end of the Pilot Peak Ridge. Therefore, I concluded to leave those lower chapters for future lessons, and go on with the easier Yosemite pages which I had already begun.

But before taking leave of those lower streams let me distinctly state, that in my opinion future investigation will uncover proofs of the existence in the earlier ages of Sierra Nevada ice, of vast glaciers which flowed to the very foot of the range.* Already it is clear that all of the upper basins were filled with ice so deep and universal that but few of the highest crests and ridges were sufficiently great to separate it into individual glaciers, many of the highest mountains having been flowed over and rounded like the bowlders in a river. Glaciers poured into Yosemite by every one of its cañons, and at a comparatively recent period of its history its northern wall, with perhaps the single exception of the crest of Eagle Cliff, was covered by one unbroken flow of ice, the several glaciers having united before they reached the wall.

September 30—Last evening I was camped in a small round glacier meadow, at the head of the easternmost tributary of the cascade. The meadow was velvet with grass, and circled with the most beautiful of all the coniferae, the Williamson spruce. I built a great fire, and the daisies of the sod rayed as if concious of a sun. As I lay on my back, feeling the presence of the trees— gleaming upon the dark, and gushing with life—coming closer and closer about me, and saw the small round sky coming down with its stars to dome my trees, I said, "Never was mountain mansion more beautiful, more spiritual; never was moral wanderer more blessedly homed." When the sun rose, my charmed walls were taken down, the trees returned to the common fund of the forest, and my little sky fused back into the measureless blue. I was left upon common ground to follow my glacial labor.

Yosemite River Basins. I followed the main Yosemite River northward, passing around the head of the second Yosemite tributary, which flowed about north-east until bent southward by the main current. About noon I came to the basin of the third ice tributary of the west rim, a place of domes which had long engaged my attention, and as I was anxious to study their

---

* Muir was mistaken here. There is no evidence that glaciers ever reached the western foothills of the Sierra Nevada.

structure, and the various moraines, &c., of the little glacier which had issued from their midst, I camped here near the foot of two of the most beautiful of the domes, in a sheltered hollow, the womb of the glacier. At the foot of these two domes are two lakes exactly alike in size and history, beautiful as any I ever beheld; first there is the crystal water center, then a yellowish fringe of Carex, which has lone arching leaves which dip to the water; then a beveled bossy border of yellow of Sphagnum moss, exactly marking the limits of the lake; further back is a narrow zone of dryer meadow, smooth and purple with grasses which grow in soft plushy sods, interrupted here and there by clumpy gatherings of blueberry bushes. The purple Kalmia grows here also, and the splendidly flowered Phyllodoce; but these are small, and weave into the sod, spreading low in the grasses and glowing with them. Besides these flowering shrubs, the meadow is lightly sprinkled with daisies, and dodecatheons and white violets, most lovely meadows devinely adjusted to most lovely lakes.

In the afternoon I followed down the bed of the tributary to its junction with the main glacier; then, turning to the right, crossed the mouths of the first two tributaries which I had passed in the morning; then, bearing east, examined a cross section of the main trunk, and reached camp by following up the north bank of the tributary. Between the three tributaries above-mentioned are well-defined medial moraines, having been preserved from leveling floods by their position on the higher slopes, with but small water-collecting basins behind them. Down by their junctions, where they were swept round by the main stream, is a large, level field of moraine matter, which, like all the drift-fields of this basin, is planted with heavy forests, composed mainly of a pine and fir (Pinus contorta, and Picea amabilis). This forest is now on fire. I wanted to pass through it, but feared the falling trees. As I stood watching the flapping flames and estimating chances, a tall blazing pine crashed across the gap which I wished to pass, and in a few minutes two more fell. This stirred a broken thought about special providences, and caused me to go around out of danger. *Pinus contorta* is very susceptible to fire, as it grows very close, in grovey thickets, and usually every tree is trickled and beaded with gum. The summit forests are almost entirely composed of this pine. *

Deer in the Valley. Emerging from this wooded moraine I found a great quantity of loose separate bowlders upon a polished hilltop, which had formed a part of the bottom of the main ice stream. They were a extraordinary size, some large as houses, and I started northward to seek the mountain from which they had been torn. I had gone but a little way when I discovered a deer quietly feeding upon a narrow strip of green meadow about sixty or seventy yards ahead of me. As the wind blew gently toward it, I thought the opportunity good for testing the truth of hunters' accounts of the deer's wonderful keeness of scent, and stood quite still, and as the deer continued to feed tranquilly, only casting round his head occasionally to drive away the flies, I began to think his nose was no better than my own, when suddenly, as if pierced by a bullet, he sprang up into the air and galloped confusedly without turning to look; but in a few seconds, as if doubtful of the direction of the danger, he came bounding back, caught a glimpse of me, and ran off a second time in a settled direction.

The Yosemite basin is a favorite summer home of the deer. The leguminous vines and juicy grasses of the great moraines supply savory food, while the many high hidings of the Hoffman Mountain, accessible by narrow passes, afford favorite shelter. Grizzly and brown bears also love Yosemite Creek. Berries of the dwarf manzanita, and acorns of the dwarf live-oak are abundant upon the dry hilltops; and these with some plants and the larvae of black ants are the favorite food of bears if varied occasionally by a stolen sheep or a shepherd. The gorges of the Tuolumne Cañon, on the north end of the basin, are their principal hiding places of this region. Higher in the range their food is not plentiful and lower they are molested by man.

On returning to camp I passed three of the domes of the north bank, and was struck by the exact similarity of their structure,

* The eastern larch, or tamarack, does not grow in California; Muir is here referring to the lodgepole pine.

the same concentric layers, with a perpendicular cleavage, but less perfectly developed and more irregular. This little dome tributary, about 2½ miles long by 1½ wide, must have been one of the most beautiful of the basin: all of its upper circling rim is adorned with domes, some half-born, sunk in the parent rock, some broken and torn up on the sides by the ice, and a few nearly perfect, from their greater strength of structure or more favorable position. The two lakes above described are the only ones of the tributary basin, both domes and lakes handiwork of the glacier.

A Glacier's Death. In the waning days of this mountain ice, when the main river began to shallow and break like a Summer cloud, its crests and domes rising higher and higher, and island rocks coming to light far out in the main current, then many a tributary died, and this one, cut off from its trunk, moved slowly back amid the gurgling and gushing of its bleeding rills, until, crouching in the shadows of this half-mile hollow, it lived a feeble separate life. Here its days come and go, and the hiding glacier lives and works. It brings bowlders and sand and fine dust polishings from its sheltering domes and cañons, building up a terminal moraine, which forms a dam for the waters which issue from it; and beneath, working in the dark, it scoops a shallow lake basin. Again the glacier retires, crouching under cooler shadows, and a cluster of steady years enables the dying glacier to make yet another moraine dam like the first; and, where the granite begins to rise in curves to form the upper dam, it scoops another lake. Its last work is done, and it dies. The twin lakes are full of pure, green water, and floating masses of snow and broken ice. The domes, perfect in sculpture, gleam in new-born purity, lakes and domes reflecting each other bright as the ice which made them. God's seasons circle on, glad brooks born of the snow and the rain sing in the rocks, and carry sand to the naked lakes, and, in the fullness of time, comes many a chosen plant; first a lowly carex with dark brown spikes, then taller sedges and rushes, fixing a shallow soil, and now comes many grasses, and daisies, and blooming shrubs, until lake and meadow growing throughout the season like a flower in Summer, develop to the perfect beauty of to-day.

How softly comes night to the mountains. Shadows grow upon all the landscape; only the Hoffman Peaks are open to the sun. Down in this hollow it is twilight, and my two domes, more impressive, than in a broad day, seem to approach me. They are not vast and over-spiritual, like Yosemite Tissiack, but comprehensible and companionable, and susceptible of human affinities. The darkness grows, and all of their finer sculpture dims. Now the great arches and deep curves sink also, and the whole structure is massed in black against the starry sky.

I have set fire to two pine logs, and the neighboring trees are coming to my charmed circle of light. The two-leaved pine, with sprays and tassles innumerable, the silver fir, with magnificent frouded whorls of shining boughs, and the graceful noddling spruce, dripping with cones, and seeming yet more spiritual in this campfire light. Grandly do my logs give back their light, slow gleaned from the suns of a hundred Summers, garnered beautifully away in dotted cells and in beads of amber gum; and, together with this outgust of light, seems to flow all the other riches of their life, and their living companions are looking down as if to witness their perfect and beautiful death. But I am weary and must rest. Good-night to my two logs and two lakes, and to my two domes high and black on the sky, with a cluster of stars between.

"Yosemite Glaciers. The Ice Streams of the Great Valley. Their Progress and Present Condition—Scenes among the Glacier Beds (From an Occasional Correspondent of the Tribune.)" *New York Tribune,* December 5, 1871, p. 8, cols. 5–6.

The last brief passage, from a journal entry of 1872, finds Muir defending his own seemingly aimless existence, his habits of wandering and roaming. But he is also fully aware that the alternative, for him, is one of conformity and drudgery.

[January 6, 1872]

Instead of narrowing my attention to bookmaking out of material I have already eaten and drunken, I would rather stand in what all the world would call an idle manner, literally gaping with all the mouths of soul and body, demanding nothing, fearing nothing, but hoping and enjoying enormously. So-called sentimental, transcendental dreaming seems the only sensible and substantial business that one can engage in.

Wolfe, ed., *John of the Mountains*, pp. 102–3.

Part Three

A Magical Person: Views of John Muir in Yosemite by Several Travelers (1870–1872)

We stopped at a sawmill where I had a pleasant talk with a handsome young Scotchman. . . . Indeed Mr. Muir was so eloquent, so unexpected, and so charming that he seemed well in harmony with the Valley.

Mrs. R. L. Waterston, 1870

Most of this book is autobiography, either overt or implicit. But this short section looks away from Muir's own words to the words of those who saw and knew him during the peak years of his Yosemite experience. The section, in fact, moves from the biographical to the fictional, ending with brief selections from the only novel which ever used Muir as a character. The observers we have selected for quotation are representative: everyone who met Muir in the early 1870s was dazzled by the glow and vigor of his intelligence.

The first of these traveler's accounts of Muir in Yosemite, describing him as a "handsome young Scotchman," was written by Mrs. R. L. Waterston of Quincy, Massachusetts, who was visiting the great west with her husband. Muir had lived in the valley only a little more than half a year when he became its interpreter for the Waterstons, but he was already speaking as an enthusiast and expert. Mrs. Waterston uses for him the revealing word "unexpected": the incongruity, for all these cultivated travelers, is to find someone so articulate in so wild a place.

Yosemite Valley, Cal.,
July 4th, 1870.

We found fair accommodations at Leidig's, the first house you reach in the Valley. Mr. Bacon's party and ourselves are the only travellers in the house. There are three hotels in the Valley. We walked through a pleasant path last evening, the little moon looked over the great Yosemite cliffs very much as she does at Quincy. This A.M. I took a walk of four miles with our Guide to the Yosemite Fall—a scramble, but the scenery worth it. We stopped at a sawmill where I had a pleasant talk with a handsome young Scotchman. His love of nature and the study of Botany is very great and after receiving an education at one of the colleges (I was going to say *western* colleges, but in California I must say Eastern) he came to California and supports himself by working as he goes, camping out alone, or rather living with Nature. He is a remarkable man—has read and studied Botany well. His love of nature, who is "his mother and divine" casts out all fear. He told me of valleys lying far beyond this, hidden away among mountains, exquisite in their beauty, filled with lovely flowers and trees and all untrodden by man—"only God is there", he said. He told me that those desolate plains we passed over between Stockton and Mariposa blossomed like the "Garden of the Lord" in the spring, worlds of

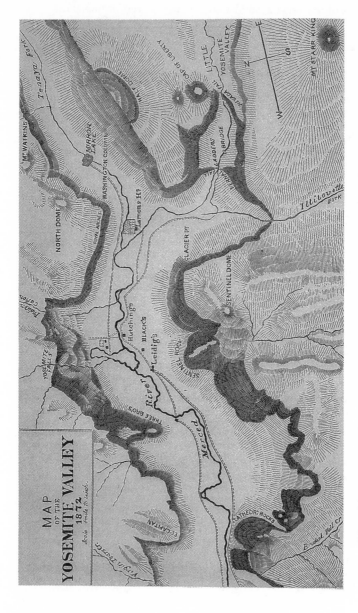

Map of the Yosemite Valley, 1872. Published in Samuel Kneeland's *Wonders of Yosemite* (Boston, 1873).

beauty and flowers. "I was keeping sheep all winter there, and in April it was more beautiful than words can tell". Indeed Mr. Muir was so eloquent, so unexpected, and so charming that he seemed well in harmony with the Valley. He is at present running a saw-mill for his daily bread and living in a little hut beside which a stream flows and flowers bloom. This description of the plains made me quite wish for a winter there, but think I am not well fitted for a shepherdess.

National Park Service, Yosemite National Park, Yosemite Collections, File 9183–C, courtesy Hanna family.

The second observer is John Erastus Lester, author of a book on the Yosemite and another, from which our selection is taken, titled *The Atlantic to the Pacific: What to See and How to See It* (1873). Lester, taking advantage of the new market opened by the transcontinental railroad, took as his form the talkative travel book. He is mistaken to say that Muir "returned home, closed up his business," but right about Muir's glacial theories: Muir was apparently arguing his position against Whitney in discussions with valley visitors as early as 1870–1871. Lester shows himself most interested in the scientific side of Muir's intelligence.

Whoever visits the Yo-Semite Valley should find and become acquainted with John Muir, the scholar and enthusiast, who has seen more of the Valley and adjacent country than any other white man. Visiting the Valley about four years ago, he became so much impressed with its grandeur and sublimity, that he returned home, closed up his business, and then took up his permanent residence here; and for three years, now, he has 'been reading this great book of nature,' as he says. Our evenings we spent in his little cabin; and one night the clock struck three in the morning before we ended what to me was a most instructive discussion, upon the different theories which have been advanced to account for the formation of the Yo-Semite.

The theory advanced by Whitney never did satisfy me; and the more I observed, the more doubts arose; and from Mr. Muir facts enough were obtained to lead me to believe with Agassiz, that all such deep-ploughed gorges have been made by immense ice-floes. It seems strange that so few of our scientific men have visited the Valley, and made a *thorough* examination; for, so far, only superficial glances have been made, and crude theories are the result. This Valley is upon so much grander a scale than any other yet found, that geologists have shrunk from advancing a theory grand enough to explain it. Until we can describe an ice-floe broader and deeper by a thousand times than any now known, and shall find its terminal moraine in the great valleys of the Sacramento and San Joaquin, we shall fail to discern in the Yo-Semite, one of Nature's grandest works.

John Erastus Lester, *The Atlantic to the Pacific: What to See and How to See It* (London: Longmans, Green, 1873), pp. 159–60.

Joseph Le Conte was one of the first professors at the young University of California. In 1870 he was approached by some students who wished to visit the Yosemite region. They began in Oakland, rode across the San Joaquin till they reached the valley, where they camped a week or so; and they returned via Tuolumne Meadows and Lake Tahoe. Our selection is taken from the *Journal of Ramblings* written by Le Conte during this trip, first published in San Francisco in 1875.

AUGUST 5.—Today to Yosemite Falls. This was the hardest day's experience yet. We thought we had plenty of time, and therefore started late. Stopped a moment at the foot of the falls, at a saw-mill, to make inquiries. Here found a man in rough miller's garb, whose intelligent face and earnest, clear blue eyes excited my interest. After some conversation, discovered that it was Mr. Muir, a gentleman of whom I had heard much from Mrs. Professor Carr and others. He had also received a letter from Mrs. Carr concerning our party, and was looking for us. We were glad to meet each other. I urged him to go with us to Mono, and he seemed disposed to do so. . . .

We commenced the ascent [of Yosemite Fall]. We first clambered up a mere pile of loose débris (talus), four hundred feet high, and inclined at least forty-five to fifty degrees. We had to keep near to one another, for the boulders were constantly loosened by the foot and went bounding down the incline until they reached the bottom. Heated and panting, we reached the top of the lower fall, drank, and plunged our heads in the foaming water until thoroughly refreshed. After remaining here nearly an hour, we commenced the ascent to the foot of the upper fall. Here the clambering was the most difficult and precarious I have ever tried: sometimes climbing up perpendicular rock faces, taking advantage of cracks and clinging bushes; sometimes along joint-cracks, on the dizzy edge of fearful precipices; sometimes over rock faces so smooth and highly inclined that we were obliged to go on hands and knees. In many places a false step would be fatal. There was no trail at all; only piles of stones here and there to mark the best route. But when at last we arrived we were amply repaid for our labor. Imagine a sheer cliff, sixteen hundred feet high, and a stream pouring over it. Actually, the water seems to fall out of the very sky itself. . . .

Coming down in the afternoon the fatigue was less, but the danger much greater. We were often compelled to slide down the face of rocks in a sitting posture, to the great detriment of the posterior portion of our trousers. Reached bottom at half-past five P.M. Here learned from Mr. Muir that he would certainly go to Mono with us. We were much delighted to hear this. Mr. Muir is a gentleman of rare intelligence, of much knowledge of science, particularly of botany, which he has made a specialty. He has lived several years in the valley, and is thoroughly acquainted with the mountains in the vicinity. A man of so much intelligence tending a sawmill!—not for himself, but for Mr. Hutchings. This is California!

AUGUST 8.—Today we leave Yosemite; we therefore got up very early, intending to make an early start. I go out again into the meadow, to take a final farewell view of Yosemite. The sun is just rising; wonderful, warm, transparent golden light (like Bierstadt's picture*) on El Capitan; the whole other side of the valley is deep, cool shade; the bald head of South Dome glistening in the distance. The scene is magnificent. . . .

Made about fourteen miles, and about 2 P.M. reached a meadow near the top of Three Brothers. Here we camped for the night in a most beautiful grove of fir—*Abies concolor* and *magnifica;* chose our sleeping-places; cut branches of spruce and

* Le Conte is here referring to the painting *Yosemite Valley* (1868).

made the most delightful elastic and aromatic beds, and spread our blankets in preparation for night. After dinner, [we] lay down on our blankets and gazed up through the magnificent tall spruces into the deep blue sky and the gathering masses of white clouds. Mr. Muir gazes and gazes, and cannot get his fill. He is a most passionate lover of nature. Plants and flowers and forests, and sky and clouds and mountains seem actually to haunt his imagination. He seems to revel in the freedom of this life. I think he would pine away in a city or in conventional life of any kind. He is really not only an intelligent man, as I saw at once, but a man of strong, earnest nature, and thoughtful, closely observing, and original mind. I have talked much with him today about the probable manner in which Yosemite was formed. He fully agrees with me that the peculiar cleavage of the rock is a most important point, which must not be left out of account. He further believes that the valley has been wholly formed by causes still in operation in the Sierra—that the Merced Glacier and the Merced River and its branches, when we take into consideration the peculiar cleavage, and also the rapidity with which the fallen and falling boulders from the cliffs are disintegrated into dust, have done the whole work. The perpendicularity is the result of cleavage; the want of talus is the result of the rapidity of disintegration and the recency of the disappearance of the glacier. I differ with him only in attributing far more to preglacial action.

Joseph Le Conte, *A Journal of Ramblings through the High Sierra of California by the University Excursion Party* (1875; reprint ed., San Francisco: Sierra Club, 1960), pp. 56–59, 66–68.

In the spring of 1871 James Bradley Thayer accompanied Ralph Waldo Emerson and ten others by train from Boston to California. He later published, in 1884, *A Western Journey with Mr. Emerson.* Thayer's account of Muir in this book recognizes that the young man tending a saw-mill in Yosemite Valley has "real intelligence and character," but also somewhat smugly finds Muir's enthusiasm for nature "amusing." Muir in his eagerness to show Emerson the truths of Yosemite had hoped to separate the old philosopher-poet from his entourage; Thayer's innocent revenge was to employ a haughty tone in his book and to refer to Muir by the initial of his name. Thus: "It was pleasant, as we rode along, to hear [Emerson] sound M. on his literary points. M. was not strong there; he preferred, for instance, Alice Cary to

Byron." Muir joined the Emerson party for a visit to the great sequoias of the Mariposa grove. (Shortly after Emerson's departure Muir wrote him the letter which appears in Part Two of this book.)

It was a sunny and pleasant ride. M. talked of the trees; and we grew learned, and were able to tell a sugar pine from a yellow pine, and to name the silver fir, and the "libocedrus," which is almost our arbor-vitae and second cousin to the great sequoia. By and by M. called out that he saw the sequoias. The general level was now about fifty-five hundred feet above the sea; the trees stood a little lower, in a hollow of the mountain. . . .

We passed along from one collection of the trees to another. Sometimes there were fifty of them near together; and then, again, they were scattered. . . . The top in the perfect tree, as M. pointed out to us, is just a parabola, and not at all the peaked shape of the pine; it is akin to the cedar and the juniper. . . .

We sat down to lunch near a hut, and had a chance to rest and to look about us more quietly. M. protested against our going away so soon: "It is," said he, "as if a photographer should remove his plate before the impression was fully made;" he begged us to stay there and camp with him for the night. After lunch Mr. Emerson, at [Galen] Clark's request, chose and named a tree. This had been done by one distinguished person and another, and a sign put up to commemorate it. Mr. Emerson's tree was not far from the hut; it was a vigorous and handsome one, although not remarkably large, measuring fifty feet in circumference at two and a half feet from the ground. He named it Samoset, after our Plymouth sachem; having at first doubted a little over Logan. He had greatly enjoyed the day. "The greatest wonder," said he, "is that we can see these trees and not wonder more."

We were off at about three o'clock, and left M. standing in the forest alone; he was to pass the night there in solitude, and to find his way back to the valley on foot. We had all become greatly interested in him, and hated to leave him. His name has since grown to be well known at the East, through his valuable articles in the magazines.

James Bradley Thayer, *A Western Journey with Mr. Emerson* (Boston: Little, Brown, 1884), pp. 88–109 passim, esp. pp. 100–102, 106–9.

As a young lad, Merrill Moores had hiked with John Muir in Wisconsin, and Muir later wrote to Moores's mother to ask that the boy, sixteen in 1872, "be sent west to spend the summer" in the Yosemite Valley. The boy traveled west on the new railroads, bought a horse in San Francisco and took it on a boat to Stockton, then rode inland to the Valley "to Black's Hotel, where I met John Muir, looking as young and really handsomer than he had looked on our Wisconsin ramble, in 1867." Muir had seven saddle-horses from a rancher in the San Joaquin Valley, but "knew nothing about and cared even less for horses, regarding them as a necessary nuisance"; so Moores was given the job of caring for these animals, "a great treat to me, and to put them in my charge was a real relief to John Muir." The two brief selections from Moores describe a scientific expedition to the Mt. Lyell glacier, and a parting-scene on a mountain trail; Moores plausibly imitates Muir's dialect in a characteristic sentence on being "a great mon." Later Moores represented his Indianapolis district in the U.S. Congress, and served on the National Parks Committee at his own request: Muir's wilderness ethics were clearly a formative influence.

Muir wished to examine the glacier near the top of Mount Lyell, the tallest mountain in the vicinity of the Yosemite, the top of which had been pronounced inaccessible by the surveyors and other authorities. I accompanied him. Starting early in the morning on our horses, we made our way around Half Dome to Tenaya Creek and followed it up as far as Soda Springs, where the purest of cold water pours forth from the earth, heavily charged with carbonic-acid gas. At night, we tethered our horses with long lariats and built a fire to keep off the coyotes—keeping it up, of course, all night—and lay down to sleep, each in his army blanket and pillowed on his saddle. With the morning, we breakfasted on some of my villainous sour-dough bread, which was all that we had except oatmeal, which we boiled and ate, Scotch fashion, without sugar.

Mr. Muir agreed with me that, if I would assist him to run a line of stakes across the glacier on a line drawn transversely across it at about the middle, he would go with me to see if the peak could be surmounted. We inspected the terminal moraine and both of the lateral moraines, as far up as half way. The glacier was then about a mile wide and very nearly as long. Muir sat on the lateral moraine on a huge bowlder and gave directions as I crossed the glacier driving a stake in at every hundred yards.

In October we returned and found the rate of speed of the

glacier at various points. As the straight line of stakes had become the arc of an enormous circle, we had absolute proof that it was a *living* glacier; and this was absolutely the first proof ever given that the canyons of the lower Sierra are of glacial origin. Muir had previously found other proofs, such as glacial mud at the terminal moraines; but this was the final and convincing proof; and Muir's contention as to their origin which he held alone for some years is now universally conceded.

Later, Muir and I took two eminent artists, William Keith and a Mr. Ross into the wilds of the Little Yosemite and spent a week while the artists transferred much of the exquisite and dainty beauty of that lovely reduced copy of the Yosemite to canvas. Still later, Mr. Muir, Professor Joseph Le Conte, and I went to the top of Clouds Rest. I rode all the way, up and back; but the older men walked the last half mile or so. It was late in October and I was about to leave the valley for Oregon, while Muir and Le Conte were starting east for Mono Lake. On the very apex of the magnificent mountain peak I left them, and Professor Le Conte said to me: "Well, Merrill, we have had a most delightful week together, and bidding you good-bye, I wish you a pleasant journey." John Muir held out his right hand, and said in his broad Scotch: "Weel, Merrill, ye may possibly become a great mon, and t'would nae mickle astonish me an ye do; but I assure ye, ye'll nae ever make an eminent naturalist and I wad ye'd so tell your mither."

Merrill Moores, "John Muir in Yosemite in 1872," *Sierra Club Bulletin* 23 (April 1938): 6–8.

Mrs. Carr's letter to the editor of the *Overland Monthly,* found in the Overland files at the Bancroft Library, affords another view of Muir and the Muir Circle in the early 1870s. The sentence on Muir's character deserves to be known.

Oakland, Jan. 17 [1872]

Ed. *Overland.*
    Dear Sir:
    Mr. Emerson urged me last summer to put my monthly bulletins from the YoSemite which come in private letters from

our friend and pupil *John Muir* before the public. In accordance with my request, this last letter is in readiness for the printers use. Mr. Muir has been in the Valley for three years, studying it as no other instructed person has ever done. He is as modest as he is gifted, and utterly devoid of literary ambition.

I offer this paper to the *Overland* on my own responsibility, if accepted please notify me, and if not return as early as possible to

Mrs. E. S. Carr

The Bancroft Library, University of California, Berkeley, *Overland Monthly* files, C.H. 97, Letter from J. C. Carr.

A far more idealized Muir appears as the character "Kenmuir" in Maria Teresa Longworth's novel *Zanita: A Tale of the Yo-Semite* (1872). The authoress had left her native England to escape the publicity of a sensational divorce trial. She came away with the alternate names Mrs. Yelverton and Countess Avonmore, and doubtless was able to trade on the exaggerated American respect for English titles. She was traveling alone, and highly impressionable. Except for the account of Muir in Chapters 1 and 2, her novel is deservedly forgotten: voice, plotting, and enthusiastic landscape descriptions are conventional, and even the very phrasing is throughout cast in dead romantic stereotypes. A substantial part of her brief Chapter 1 is here presented, as a way of rescuing one view of Muir in the early part of 1871: reduce the glow of these descriptions and you come very close to the look, speech, and character of Muir at this time, and to the effect he could elicit from an enthusiastic observer. The countess registers his athletic balance, his goatlike ability in rock-climbing, his "flexible form"; she notes the prophetic tone of his discourse as well as his good geological information; she admires the purity of his character. Her cover, as the speaker in the novel, is the wife of "a Professor of Geology in a College of California," traveling alone in the mountain wilderness. This narrator remarks very typically at the end of Chapter 2, when Kenmuir is her guide in the Yosemite at night: "Here was I, a lone woman having transgressed her husband's directions to await him in a civilized place, alone in the wildest part of the wild world, with a stranger—the like of whom I had never met in all my travels—wandering on an untrodden path to a habitation of which I knew next to nothing. It was certainly as extraordinary and romantic a situation as any lover of fiction could have framed." It certainly was: a perfect situation for a sexual adventure, except, of course, that the man is Kenmuir who loves the mountains and has no thought of physical love. The authoress, under the decent and literary guise of her married narrator, is plainly in love with her Kenmuir; the resulting image of John Muir is of value precisely because of this distortion.

There is evidence, in a letter Muir wrote to his brother David on December 1, 1871 (now housed with the Muir Papers), that Muir himself had a hand in the novel's actual writing. What he contributed is unclear, but it is very unlikely that the descriptions of Yosemite scenery are his: Muir's own writing is more lively and precise than this. Our passage begins when the professor's wife is approaching the Yosemite with her guide, Horse-shoe Bill.

We rode from early morn until even through the most glorious country it had ever been my fate to traverse. Mountain rose above mountain, and tower above tower of rocky peaks; and, away up, mingling with the snowy clouds, peered the no less snowy caps of the distant Sierra Nevadas. Here and there we could see green valleys nestling in among the mountains, and deep cañons filled with dark pines.

"O, them's nowhar to the Valley whar I'm agoin' to take you; and we can most see some of it now. Them three peaks as you see a topplin' over one another, a sort of playin' leap-frog, the Indians call Pom-pom-pas-us."

Looking in the direction to which he pointed, I beheld a chaos of mountain tops and deep chasms, all seemingly thrown inextricably together, and apparently inaccessible. My heart began to fail me as to my further progress, when a peculiar looking object foreign to the scenery caught my eye.

"What on earth is that?" I exclaimed, reining up my not unwilling mustang, and pointing to the singular creature extending itself as though about to take wing from the very verge of a pinnacle overhanging a terrific precipice. "Is it a man, or a tree, or a bird?"

"It's a man, you bet," replied my guide, chuckling. "No tree or shrub as big as my fist ever found footing there. It's that darned idiot Kenmuir, and the sooner he dashes out that rum mixture he calls brains the sooner his troubles'll be over, that's my idea."

"It's not mine though," I said decisively, "for if he is really crazy we are the more bound to take care of him. Suppose you give a shrill whistle to attract his attention."

"He'll not bother for that, he'll know it's me; but if you ride around this here point he'll see you belike; that'll be a novel sight for him," said the guide, who was by no means an ill-natured man: only thoroughly imbued with a recklessness of human life, which years spent in the wildwood seems to engender in the most humane.

Adopting his suggestion, we quickly rounded the point, when the singular figure was seen swaying to and fro with extended arms as if moved by the wind, the head thrown back as in swimming, and the long brown hair falling wildly about his face and neck.

The point on which he stood was a smooth jutting rock only a few inches in width, and a stone thrown over it would fall vertically into the valley five thousand feet below. My heart beat fast with horrible dread as my guide cooly explained this fact to me. I hardly dared to fix my eyes upon the figure lest I should see it disappear, or remove them, lest it should be gone when I looked again. In my desperation, I extended that power of will which is said to convey itself through space without material aid. I strove to communicate with him by intangible force. The charm seemed to work well. He turned quickly towards me, and, with a spring like an antelope, was presently on *terra firma* and approaching us.

"There, you'll have plenty on him now," said Horseshoe Bill. "He loafs about this here valley gatherin' stocks and stones, as I may say, to be Scriptural, and prasin' the Lord for makin' of him sech a born fool. Well some folks is easy satisfied!"

As the lithe figure approached, skipped over the rough boulders, poising with the balance of an athlete, or skirting a shelf of rock with the cautious activity of a goat, never losing for a moment the rhythmic motion of his flexile form, I began to think that his attitude on the overhanging rock might not, after all, have been so chimerical; and my resolves, as to how I should treat this phase of insanity, began to waver very sensibly, and I fell back on that mental rear-guard,—good intentions; but when he stood before me with a pleasant "Good day, madam," my perplexity increased ten-fold, for his bright intelligent face revealed no trace of insanity, and his open blue eyes of honest questioning, and glorious auburn hair might have stood as a portrait of the angel Raphael. His figure was about five feet nine, well knit, and bespoke that active grace which only trained muscles can assume.

The guide increased my confusion by exclaiming, "Hello, Kenmuir! The lady wants to speak to you."

I wished the guide at Jericho for giving me such false notions. Why had he induced me to believe this man a raving maniac, only to compel me, like Old Dogberry, to write myself down an ass. I could have as soon reproached one of the clouds gyrating round the crest of the mountain with running into danger.

"Can I do anything for you?" asked Kenmuir gently.

"She wants to know what you were doing out on that bloody knob overhanging etarnity?"

"Praising God," solemnly replied Kenmuir.

"Thought that would start him," interrupted the guide.

"Praising God, madam, for his mighty works, his glorious earth, and the sublimity of these fleecy clouds, the majesty of that great roaring torrent," pointing to the Nevada, "that leaps from rock to rock, in exultant joy, and laves them, and kisses them with caresses of downiest foam. O, no mother ever pressed her child in tenderer embrace, or sung to it in more harmonious melody; and my soul joins in with all this shout of triumphant gladness, this burst of glorious life; this eternity of truth and beauty and joy; rejoices in the gorgeous canopy above us, in the exquisite carpet with which the valley is spread of living, palpitating, breathing splendor. Hearken to the hymn of praise which resounds upwards from every tiny sedge, every petal and calyx of myriads and myriads of flowers, all perfect, all replete with the divine impress of Omnipotent power. Shall man alone by silent and callous? Come, madam, let me lead you to Pal-li-li-ma, the point I have just left, where you can have a more complete view of this miracle of nature, for I am sure you also can worship in this temple of our Lord."

Here was a pretty fix for a Professor's wife, and a sensible woman! I was about to put myself in the identical situation which but a few moments before had induced me to consider the man who occupied it a lunatic.

Horse-shoe Bill remarked my puzzled expression, and

laughed, "Ho, he'll guide you right enough; he knows every inch
of the road as well as I do. You needn't be afeard; he'll take you
to the shanty I told you of, where you can locate for the night,
and I'll make tracks back agin, if so be you don't want me."

One thought of the maniac shot through my mind, not as a
fear, but a souvenir. I looked on the face of Kenmuir, shining
with a pure and holy enthusiasm, and it reminded me of the face
of a Christ I had seen years ago in some little old Italian village;
not a picture of any note, but possessing such a tender, loving,
benignant expression, that I had never forgotten it; and had then
thought that the artist must have intended it for the Salvator
Mundi before he became the Man of Sorrows.

With this picture brought forcibly to my mind, I resigned
myself cheerfully, and followed his lead to the great projecting
rock called the Glacier Point, or Pal-li-li-ma, where I had first
seen him, and where there are still traces of ancient glaciers,
which he said "are no doubt the instruments the Almighty used
in the formation of this valley."

As we proceeded slowly and carefully, my thoughts dwelt
with deep interest on the individual in advance of me. Truly his
garments had the tatterdemalion style of a Mad Tom. The waist
of his trousers was eked out with a grass band; a long flowing
sedge rush stuck in the solitary button-hole of his shirt, the
sleeves of which were ragged and forlorn, and his shoes appeared to have known hard and troublous times. What if he had
been at some previous period, insane, and still retained the
curious mania of believing that human beings might through
righteousness float in ambient air? What if he should insist on
our making the experiment this evening together? What would
my husband say if he knew all, and saw me here committed to
the sole care of this man with the beautiful countenance, and
with no other guarantee, in a wilderness of mighty rocks,
gigantic trees, and awful precipices, a hundred miles from
anywhere! . . .

But, in the course of conversation with my *cicerone,* I soon
divined that his refinement was innate, his education collegiate,
not only from his scientific treatment of his subject, but his
correct English. Kenmuir, I decided in my mind, was a gen-

tleman; and behind this bold rampart I resolved to intrench myself against the sarcastic tiltings of the Professor.

As we approached the point, Kenmuir said with a gleeful laugh, "I do not intend to take you out on the overhanging rock, where I was standing, but to a very nice little corner, where you can sit your horse comfortably, unless you really want to dismount."

. . . "These are the Lord's fountains," said Kenmuir, clasping his hands in the intensity of his delight, "and away up above, elevated amid clouds, are the crests of the God-like peaks covered with eternal snows. These are the reservoirs whence He pours his floods to cheer the earth, to refresh man and beast, to lave every sedge and tiny moss; from those exalted pinnacles flow the source of life, and joy, and supreme bliss to millions of breathing things below; to the dreamy-eyed cattle that you see four thousand feet in the valley beneath us, standing knee-deep in the limpid pool; to the tiny insects that are skimming in ecstatic merriment around every glistening ribbon of water as it falls. Look! and see those silvery threads of water all hurrying down so swiftly, yet so gracefully, to bathe the upturned face of nature, and varnish with new brilliancy her enameled breast. Beyond is the Lord's workshop. With these resistless glaciers he formed a royal road.—from the heights of the topmost Sierras which you now see covered with snow, roseate from the sun's last beams.—into the valley at our feet. Yet all is lovely in form, and harmonious in color. Look at that ledge of rock—the hardest of granite—how exquisitely it is tapestried with helianthemum. Would you like a bunch?"

And before I could reply, the rash man had leapt down, and alighted like a bird on a perch, and grasped a bunch of ferns, which he stroked affectionately, and carefully stowed away in the grass cincture, whilst there was but a half foot of rock between him and "etarnity," as the guide expressed it.

Thérèse Yelverton (Viscountess Avonmore), *Zanita: A Tale of the Yo-Semite* (New York: Hurd and Houghton, 1872), pp. 3–8, 8–9.

Part Four

Visionary Science (1871–1872)

Nature is a flood and we are all in it.
John Muir, Muir Papers, undated

By the spring of 1872 it was plainly evident that Muir could make a living as a writer. Yet he continued to pour most of his efforts into letters and notebooks, at last prompting Mrs. Carr to warn against further delay in article- and book-making. The success of the *Tribune* piece made it clear that he could, if he wished, turn out more manuscripts of the scientific-narrative variety, and that they would find a market, but if Muir sensed it was time to publish his work, he expressed to her confusion on how to begin: "All say 'write,' but I don't know how or what." Carr lent advice: Use quality paper, coarse and lined, and a broad pen, and begin!

On New Year's Day Muir set down some thoughts of a recent storm and sent the manuscript to Mrs. Carr. The following month he mailed to her letters on bears, coyotes, and Twenty Hill Hollow. Mrs. Carr, in turn, acting as a sort of literary agent, hand-carried these manuscripts to the editor of the *Overland* who began placing them in the monthly magazine. He was soon asking for more articles from "Mr. Muir the Poet," as Carr sometimes called her protégé.

The following two letters discuss these manuscripts, and with the journal entries give some idea of Muir's thoughts about his writing career and his place in the wilderness and in society. However successful his articles might be, and whatever reputation as a scientist he might be gaining among the "learned," he evidently continued to feel isolated, bashful, and a misfit—a man, as he writes, who did not "mould in with the rest of mankind." These letters may also be read for hints of Muir's later conservationist ethic. The first letter is to Mrs. Carr; the second is to Emily Pelton.

Yosemite Valley
February 13, 1872

Your latest letter is dated December 31st. I see that some of our letters are missing. I received the box and ate the berries and Liebig's extract long ago and told you all about it, but Mrs. Yelverton's book, and magazine articles* I have not yet seen. Perhaps they may come next mail. How did you send them? I sympathize with your face and your great sorrows, but you will bathe in the fountain of light, life, and love of our mountains and be healed. And here I wish to say that when you and Al and the Doctor come, I wish to be completely free. Therefore let me know that you will certainly come and *when*. I will gladly cut off a slice of my season's time however thick—the thicker the

---

* Several of her short articles appeared in the *Overland Monthly*. The book referred to is *Zanita: A Tale of the Yo-Semite*.

better—and lay it aside for you. I am in the habit of asking so many to *come, come, come* to the mountain baptisms that there is danger of having others on my hands when you come, which must not be. I will mark off one or two or three months of bare, dutiless time for our blessed selves or the few good and loyal ones that you may choose. Therefore, at the expense even of breaking a dozen of civilization's laws and fences, I want you to *come*. For the high Sierra the months of July, August, and September are best.

As for your Asiatic sayings, I would gladly creep into the Vale of Casmere or any other grove upon our blessed star. I feel my poverty in general knowledge and will travel some day. You need not think that I feel Yosemite to be all in all, but more of this when you come.

I am going to send you with this a few facts and thoughts that I gathered concerning Twenty Hill Hollow, which I want to publish, if you think you can mend them and make them into a lawful article fit for *outsiders*. Plant gold is fading from California faster than did her placer gold, and I wanted to save the memory of that which is laid upon Twenty Hills.

Also I will send you some thoughts that I happened to get for poor persecuted, twice damned Coyote. If you think anybody will believe them, have them published.* Last mail I sent you some manuscript about bears and storms, which you will believe if no one else will. An account of my preliminary rambles among the glacier beds was published in the "Daily Tribune" of New York, Dec. 9th.† Have you seen it? If you have, call old Mr. Stebbin's attention to it. He will read [it] with some pleasure. Where is the old friend? I have not heard from him for a long time. Remember me to the Doctor and the boys and all my old friends.

Yours, etc.,
JOHN MUIR

John Muir, *Letters to a Friend: Written to Mrs. Ezra S. Carr, 1866–1879,* ed. William Frederic Badè (Boston: Houghton Mifflin, 1915; reprint ed., Dunwoody, Georgia: Norman S. Berg, 1973), pp. 111–13.

* The article on coyotes was never published and is presumably lost.
† Muir was mistaken; the date of publication was December 5.

Yosemite Valley
Feb. 19th [1872]

Dear Friend Emily,

I was really glad to hear from you. I wrote you at least two letters since receiving yours of last Spring. I began to fear that I had lost you all together.

I am glad to hear that you are coming here next season. You will be sure to find me without any trouble. I have never had any pictures of myself since that of yours which I suppose is the one I let Mrs. Pelton have. You will find me at Blacks Hotel. I left Mr. Hutchings because he was not kind to me. I am in every way independent & will be most happy to see you & help you to see Yosemite. You will require no photograph to know me, the most suntanned & round shouldered & bashful man of the crowd (if you catch me in a crowd), that's me. I will be here for some years, as last fall I began a careful study of the ancient glacier system of this portion of the Sierra for the Boston Academy of Science.

A sort of preliminary survey of the glacial basin of Yosemite Creek was published in the New York Tribune of December 9th (Daily) wh will give you some idea of the manner in wh my life is spent. Some winter letters of mine may also appear in the Tribune as soon as the snow blockade is broken. Last Dec' we had a glorious jubilee of waterfalls, of wh I wrote an account. It will probably appear in next month's "Overland."* If it does I hope you will see it. How gladly I would welcome Mrs. Pelton here & see Fannie who would be half a woman ere this. I would like to see you all. How fast those yrs have flown. How you must laugh at the memories of my odd appearance among you all. I remember rebuking you & Mrs. Lovewell without mercy for *Dilby chat*. Old Mrs. Newton too for irreverence & all of you for sins of some kind or another, & something else I remember, Emily—your kind words to me the first day I saw you. Kind words are likely to live in any human soil, but planted in the breast of a Scotchman they are absolutely immortal, &

---

* "Yosemite Valley in Flood," *Overland Monthly* 8 (April 1872): 347–60, reprinted below in this volume.

whatever Heaven may have in store for you in after years you have at least one friend while John Muir lives.

Remember me warmly to Mrs. Pelton & N. A. Wright. I am sorry to learn the death of Mrs. Newton — — —.

Had I been able to leave Yosemite I should have seen you ere this but Heaven keeps me to my mountain task with an iron grip loving though it be.

Do you remember Prof Carrs wife? She was at Mondell once or twice. She was friendly to me while I was a student and ever afterwards. Professor Carr is now connected with the Cal State University; they have sent me many pressing invitations to spend winter with them, but as I said I am rockbound.

In all these years since I saw you I have been isolated somehow. I don't mould in with the rest of mankind and have become far more confusedly bashful than when I lived in Mondell. Now Emily, there is a whole letter all about myself, which is a literary sin that I have not commited for some time.

Farewell, ever heartily yours
JOHN MUIR

State Historical Society of Wisconsin, Madison, SC185, "Letters and Poems, 1861–1914, written by John Muir to Emily Pelton and her mother, Mrs. F. N. Pelton of Prairie du Chien, Wis."

We have selected the following four "Autobiographical Fragments" from a heretofore unpublished manuscript, because they capture so well Muir's enthusiasm for wilderness facts, and because they emphasize the way Muir's quest for information was always accompanied by a lyric tone of voice.

It was here I first commenced my studies on earth sculpture. Everyone must study here more or less so striking are the phenomena presented—so interesting the questions we can no more cease studying than breathing, like a healthy body every healthy mind is hungry and intellectual bread is never awanting however scarce the other kind at times. We never get above the bread line—mental bread. The faintest lines of study faithfully traced lead to plainer ones and by easy steps we at length gain heights with far-reaching views.

Rocks have a kind of life perhaps not so different from ours as we imagine. Anyhow their material beauty is only a veil covering spiritual beauty—a divine incarnation—instonation.

Watch the sunbeams pouring over the forests awakening the flowers, feeding them every one, warming, reviving the myriads of the air, setting countless wings in motion—making diamonds of dewdrops, lakes silvery, painting the spray of falls in rainbow colors. Enjoy the great night like a day, hinting the eternal and imperishable in nature amid the transient and material.

In the calm morning I happened to look thru my pocket lens at one of the drops while admiring a dew-laden alder bush and was delighted to find the landscape in it in miniature—hills, trees, bushes, everything within sight, in infinitely fine lines, colors and all. Since then I never see a dewy morning or rainy day without contemplating the wonderful multiplication of the beauty of their fairy miniatures.

Muir Papers, University of the Pacific, Stockton, California, "Autobiographical Fragments," undated, File 37.14.

Among the scientists who had rambled with Muir around Yosemite's cliffs were John Runkel and Samuel Kneeland, both of the Massachusetts Institute of Technology. The pair expressed interest in Muir's glacial studies and encouraged him to send them his manuscripts,—this despite the fact the two remained somewhat skeptical of Muir's theses, and of his argument that "living glaciers" still inhabited the shadowed walls of many Yosemite canyons. Muir began a correspondence with them, and Kneeland read portions of these letters to the Boston Society of Natural History. In the letter to Mrs. Carr, presented above, Muir expressed his desire to preserve at least a memory of the endangered "plant gold" of California; in his letter to Kneeland, reproduced in the minutes of the Boston Society of Natural History, he again notes with sadness that California's beauty was "fast fading before the plough and the cattle and the herds of civilization."

March 6, 1872

The President in the chair. Twenty-one persons present.

Dr. Kneeland read the following extracts from letters written by Mr. John Muir, on the winter phenomena of the Yosemite Valley.

On the cold, south, or eclipsed side of the valley, average from January 1 to 24, 1872, at Black's Hotel:

Average morning temperature . . . . 32° Fahr.
"   noon   "   . . . . 40°5
Maximum morning   "   . . . . 36°
"   noon   "   . . . . 52°
Minimum morning   "   . . . . 22°
"   noon   "   . . . . 32°

Mild and delightful weather, wholly unlike the stormy December, with a little rain and snow, but mostly sunshine.

From Jan. 25 to Feb. 14, 1872

Average sunrise temperature at Black's . .   28°.92 Fahr.
"   noon   "   . . . . 40°.57
Maximum morning   "   . . . . 37°
Minimum morning   "   . . . . 23°
Maximum noon   "   . . . . 49°
Minimum   "   "   . . . . 34°
Rainfall during period   . . . . 237 inches [?]
Snowfall during period   3   "
Three days rainy, 3 cloudy, 2 snowy, 10 bright and clear.

January 24th, a terrible wind storm, coming from the north, the only direction in which a gale can enter this deep valley; bending and swaying the great pines two hundred feet high, usually so unbending, like a field of wheat, and showering their cones about like hailstones. The struggle of the Upper Yosemite fall, considerably swelled by the melting snows, was very beautiful; the wind seemed to surround it with a vast whirlpool, which tore it and scattered it about like folds of white drapery, now and then laying bare the black rocks behind. In the afternoon, the whole column was suddenly arrested in its descent about midway; it was not blown upward or bent to either side but towered in mid air, widening at the base, and doubtless turned inward toward the rock; it remained in this shape about three minutes, an irregular white cone, eight hundred feet high, stationary at the bottom, as if at the base the laws of gravitation had been suddenly suspended; then all at once it resumed its usual appearance. The force of the wind, and the natural inward air current behind the fall, were so strong as to bend the whole volume of water and curl it backward and inward, giving to the eye the appearance above described. Grand as are the Yosemite waterfalls, the Yosemite air-falls and cascades, masters even of the waters, are still more grand and wonderful.

This great storm produced no serious damage, prostrating only about a score of trees, breaking off many branches, and scattering the pine tassels and cedar plumes far and wide, and by this natural pruning exercising a beneficial influence upon the forests.

Erroneous views prevail as to the severity of the winter climate in this valley. On February 14, 1872, frogs croaked at night in the meadow shallows; upon the warm slopes of the north wall young grasses were an inch high, the sterile aments of the alders were ripe, the cedars were sowing their pollen, the early willows pushing out their catkins, azalea buds opening, flies and moths sporting in the sunshine, and ants busy about their spring work. The contrast between the north and south sides of the valley is remarkable; while on the north and sunny side it was spring, on the south side there were twelve inches of snow and midwinter— the two seasons separated only by half a mile of valley.

The latter part of January there was a magnificent ice cone two hundred feet high at the base of the upper Yosemite fall. This cone was about six hundred feet in diameter at the base, truncated, with the side next the wall deeply flattened; into its tolerably regular mouth, as into the crater of a volcano, poured whole columns of water which escaped by several irregular openings at the base. The rock behind the fall is dark-colored, but on both sides it is covered during frosty nights by frozen spray to a depth of from two inches to several feet; the width of this silvery edging of ice varies with the height, being greatest at the bottom and tapering to the top, like the fall to which it belongs. This grand ice creation, two hundred feet wide at the bottom, developed in a night, dies in a day; a few minutes after the sun falls upon its ragged blocks from a few pounds to several tons in weight begin to fall off, which in their fall echo through the valley like explosions of powder. The intervals of quiet which separate these explosions are from a few seconds to ten or twelve minutes; it sometimes happens that the sun disintegrates this ice before noon, but usually almost all day is required. The thundering and clattering of this falling ice are the common winter sounds, and the constant accompaniments of pleasant days. The ice cone is thus seen to be simply an accumulation of spray ice, solidified by pressure; it frequently attains a height of four or five hundred feet.

Tourists in California never see, and even the residents know nothing of, the magnificent vegetation of the great central plain of California; it is almost always remembered as a scorched and dust-clouded waste, treeless and dreary as the deserts along the Pacific Railroad. The foot-hills are smooth and flowing, and come down to the bottom levels in beautiful curves; their flowers do not occur singly or scattered about in the grass, but close together in companies, acres and hill-sides in extent, with their white, yellow and purple colors separate, yet harmoniously blending, as their fragrance is exquisite. Throughout the passes abound dogwood and alders, violets and ferns of great beauty. After passing the summit of the hills you come to the magnificent flower bed of the California plains, four hundred miles long and thirty miles wide, a great level ocean of flowers bounded by the snow-capped Sierras, watered by the San Joaquin and Sacramento Rivers. The richness of this flower garden is almost beyond belief judged by ordinary standards, or even by that of Florida, the land of flowers; for every flower inhabiting Florida, on equal areas more than a hundred grow here. The flowers are not in the grasses, as on the prairies of Illinois, but the grasses are among the flowers. One actually wades in flowers, hundreds touching the feet at every step. But all this beauty is fast fading before the plough and the cattle and herds of civilization.

February and March are the spring time of the plain, April the summer and May the autumn. Spring opens early, prepared by the rains which begin in December; between May and December rains are very rare, and this is the winter of the plain, a winter of heat and drought. By the middle of May the flowers here are dead, and the leaves dry and parched; not slowly perishing, but suddenly dying before they can fade, standing erect and un-decayed, with their beautiful urn-like seed vessels.

As you ascend from the sunny winter of the plain, you find another summer in the foot-hills of the Sierra; higher up another spring, and on the edge of the valley a snowy winter; descending into the Yosemite Valley, you find another spring, and then glorious summer along the banks of the Merced. Thus, in the space of a week, you pass through all the seasons in this remarkable region.

Proceedings of the Boston Society of Natural History (Boston: Printed for the Society, 1872–73), 15:148–51.

During the fall of 1871 Muir had quit Hutchings's sawmill and was devoting near full time to his studies and to his writing. He lived the winter of 1871–1872 at Black's Hotel but by the spring had constructed for himself his second cabin, this one on the sunny, north side of the valley at the base of the Royal Arches. With a resolve to remain free of conventions, and with a measure of financial independence gained from the *Tribune* article, he engaged himself in a near frenzy of hikes and climbs around the Yosemite's high eastern peaks. Often carrying two journals at a time—and writing into whichever one was handy—he would later shape his notes into letters and articles.

Some letters invited close friends to join him in the valley (see the next, sent to Emily Pelton); others were more formal, scientific narratives (to Samuel Kneeland); and some were personal and warm (to his sister Sarah's little boy).

Yosemite Valley
April 2, 1872

Dear Friend Emily:

Your broad pages are received. You must never waste letter time in apologies for size. The more vast and prairie-like the better. But now for the business part of your coming. Be sure you let me know within a few days the time of your setting out so that I may be able to keep myself in a findable, discoverable place. I am, as perhaps I told you, engaged in the study of glaciers and mountain structure, etc., and I am often out alone for weeks where you couldn't find me. Moreover, I have a good many friends of every grade who will be here, all of whom have greater or lesser claims on my attention. With Professor LeConte

I have made arrangements for a long scientific ramble back in the summits; also with Mrs. Carr. You will readily understand from these engagements and numerous other probabilities of visits, especially from scientific friends who almost always take me *out of* Yosemite, how important it is that I should know very nearly the time of your coming. I would like to have a week of naked, unoccupied time to spend with you and nothing but unavoidable, unescapable engagements will prevent me from having such a week.

If Mr. Knox would bring his team you could camp out, and the expense would be nothing, hardly, and you could make your headquarters at a cabin I am building. This would be much the best mode of traveling and of seeing the Valley. Independence is nowhere sweeter than in Yosemite. People who come here ought to abandon and forget all that is called business and duty, etc.; they should forget their individual existences, should forget they are born. They should as nearly as possible live the life of a particle of dust in the wind, or of a withered leaf in a whirlpool. They should come like thirsty sponges to imbibe without rule. It is blessed to lean fully and trustingly on Nature, to experience, by taking to her a pure heart and unartificial mind, the infinite tenderness and power of her love.

You mention the refining influences of society. Compared with the intense purity and cordiality and beauty of Nature, the most delicate refinements and cultures of civilization are gross barbarisms.

As for the rough vertical animals called men, who occur in and on these mountains like sticks of condensed filth, I am not in *contact* with them; I do not live with them. I live alone, or, rather, with the rocks and flowers and snows and blessed storms; I live in blessed mountain *light,* and love nothing less pure. You'll find me rough as the rocks and about the same color—granite. But as for loss of pure-mindedness that you seem to fear, come and see my teachers; come, see my Mountain Mother, and you will be at rest on that point.

We have had a glorious storm of the kind called earthquake. I've just been writing an account of it for the New York

"Tribune."* It would seem strange that any portion of our perpendicular walls are left unshattered. It is delightful to be trotted and dumpled on our Mother's mountain knee. I hope we will be blessed with some more. The first shock of the morning of [March] 26th, at half-past two o'clock, was the most sublime storm I ever experienced.

Most cordially yours,
JOHN MUIR

William Frederic Badè, *The Life and Letters of John Muir* 2 vols. (Boston: Houghton Mifflin, 1923–24), 1:323–26.

Muir's article on the great Inyo Earthquake of 1872, which he sent to the *Tribune,* was evidently never published. Another account survives, however, in the minutes of the Boston Society of Natural History:

May 15, 1872

The President in the chair. Thirty-three persons present.

Dr. S. Kneeland read extracts from a letter from Mr. John Muir, on the effects of the earthquake of March 26, 1872, in the Yosemite Valley.

"The earthquake storm in the Yosemite began Tuesday, March 26, 1872, at 2½ A.M. People were shaken out of bed, and the floors shook like the deck of a vessel at sea. First shock lasted about three minutes and with great energy and motion, undiminished to the end. For the first minute no sound but the agitation of the trees. Expected 'Sentinel Rock,' a high isolated pinnacle, would fall, but at last from the south side of the valley opposite Yosemite falls, there came a tremendous sound. Eagle Rock had fallen two thousand feet, and was pouring in an avalanche of boulders over precipices, and through forests of fir and spruce, filling the valley with a smoke of fire and rock dust,

* Badè footnotes here in *Life and Letters* that the article on earthquakes appeared in the May 7, 1872, issue, a belief repeated by Linnie Marsh Wolfe in her biography *Son of the Wilderness.* A check of the *Tribune* for that date failed, however, to turn up any article by Muir. Presumably the date May 7 is the one on which Muir sent the article to the newspaper; evidently it was never published and is lost.

and countless reverberations and echoes. Sky clear and moon bright, so that the outlines of the rocks, trees and meadows could be plainly seen; trees greatly agitated, in strange, indeterminate, motions; frogs silenced for the time, but before the dust had settled, or the echoes had died away, an owl began to hoot from the very edge of the fallen rocks, as if unconscious of any extraordinary disturbance. River soon after was found to be muddy from portions of its banks shaken into it, but otherwise flowed peacefully, in the same direction, as ever. Upper Yosemite did not seem to show the slightest agitation.

"First shock followed at intervals of a few minutes by sharp concussions, each attended by gentle undulations and by occasional smooth rumbling sounds from deep in the mountains, in a northern direction, not always readily distinguishable from the heavy sounds formed at the foot of the Upper Yosemite. Second well defined shock about an hour after first, followed by another rock avalanche from the region of Eagle Rock. A third severe shock, a few minutes after sunrise, in which the movements were less sharp and quick, and a few lateral and vertical joltings, followed by a series of short undulations or quiverings, causing the light-branched and leafless oaks to whip their upper branches as if struck by a powerful force near the ground.

"Rocks of size of thirty feet in diameter downward, coming to rest at a long rough slope at the foot of the vertical wall, covering a portion of a larger slope made centuries ago, destroyed a great number of trees, firs, pines, spruces, maples, laurels, etc., filling the air with a balsamic fragrance from their bruised trunks and branches. Trees four feet in diameter broken clear across in lengths of ten to fifteen feet, and cast in drifts like straws; others battered and flattened like crushed sugar canes; some had their tops cut smoothly off seventy to nine hundred feet from the ground by large fragments bounding above the main avalanche like the spray of a water fall.

"Other avalanches occurred in Indian Cañon, on the west side of the Cap of Liberty, and in Illilouette Cañon. The walls were not more changed by this earthquake than Mirror Lake by a passing storm. Only visible changes, a few whitish, fresh rock patches on the dark walls, and a new small rock front, capped with spires, where Eagle Rock fell. The day following was cool and calm and bright; animate nature appeared the same; some two or three [persons] were frightened out of the valley. Innumerable shocks during the 26th to 27th, but not more than fifty were noticeable, unless by persons watching for them.

"First shock by far the most severe. Watched the movements of a pail of water for hours. Noticed vibrations of considerable regularity in a north and south direction, seeming to be produced by impulses from the north acting horizontally, with the velocity of a blow. North and south vibrations constantly interrupted by impulses which seemed to proceed mostly from an easterly direction. A few circular, twisting motions were noticed; the surface of the water also at times dimpled and trembled as if receiving a succession of sharp blows from below. The rumbling under-mountain sounds were distinctly heard by everybody in the valley, and always as coming from the north."

Proceedings of the Boston Society of Natural History, 15:185–86.

Among Muir's gifts as a writer was the ability to shape his writing to his audience: the following is a personal note to a nephew which, in contrast to the scientific narratives sent to Boston, warmly reveals Muir's love for wild things, in terms and phrases a young boy can understand.

Yosemite Valley
April 25, 1872

Dear Nephew George Galloway:

I got your letter and read it twice. I like letters when they are written by farmers' boys for then they are always full of something that smells like hay and wheat and fresh butter and milk and they always seem to be tanned brown with sunshine. I think your description of the long shining tailed peacocks is first-rate. You are going to make a grand scholar. I'm glad you like your wild cats and dogs. I like all things that are wild better than tame things. God takes care of everything that is wild but he only half takes care of tame things.

A man shot a lynx in this valley last winter. Wild cats are thick here in the rocks and bushy thickets. Bears come to the valley sometimes. A man shot one here last fall and a hunter by the name of Duncan shot 59 bears not far from here in ten years. I know a cañon north from here that is full of big bears. They eat acorns and manzanita berries. Last fall I was far and high in the mountains and my bread was done and I got only a handfull of crumbs for my dinner and at night after climbing hard all day had to lie down on the rocks without any supper and in the morning had to climb up again without any breakfast, and about noon I found some manzanita berries and ate a whole lot, like a bear, and at night I got to Yosemite and found plenty to eat, and then I took a long rest and went up to the mountains again. Some day I think you'll come up here to see the waterfalls and the high rocks. Good-night. From your uncle John who always loves you.

Muir Papers, *Correspondence,* Box 14, Letters Sent, 1860–1873.

The letter which Muir sent to Mrs. Carr on the first of January, which he termed "A Jubilee of Waters," she delivered to the *Overland Monthly* with the note we have reproduced in Part Three. The magazine published it three months later as "Yosemite Valley in Flood"; it was so well received that before the year was over the *Overland* published two other of his manuscripts. By the following year they referred to Muir as their "leading contributor."

Essays about the natural world have seldom, before or since, been more ardent. Muir's method is everywhere to attribute to the Yosemite scene varying degrees of life and consciousness: the Merced River, for example, is a "she" and is "readable." The affinity between mind and world is so close that Muir as observer speaks of himself "seeing and listening as every pore," not so much perceiving as—something more primordial—absorbing the landscape. Often in this language the distinction between subject and object is knowingly obliterated, and the personality of Muir as speaker-hero is displaced into a series of mountain objects. The prose is obsessed with the procedures of transition and contiguity, as it follows the voyage of self in scene. Objects in the world of reference become second selves. And yet, to see our own vital force objectified is not, for Muir, to wish to dominate the external scene, whose otherness is always acknowledged. The world is appropriated only through prose, and thus left alone; but this is a lot to ask of mere prose, nothing less than the reconstitution of the reader's sense of fact and of sight.

Yosemite Valley in Flood

Many a joyful stream is born in the Sierras, but not one can sing like the Merced. In childhood, high on the mountains, her silver thread is a moving melody; of sublime Yosemite she is the voice; the blooming *chaparral* or the flowery plains owe to her fullness their plant-wealth of purple and gold, and to the loose dipping willows and broad green oaks she is bounteous in blessing. I think she is the most absorbing and readable of rivers. I have lived with her for three years, sharing all her life and fortunes, dreaming that I appreciated her; but I never have so much as imagined the sublimity, the majesty of her music, until seeing and listening at every pore I stood in her temple to-day.

December brought to Yosemite, first of all, a cluster of ripe, golden days, and silvery nights—a radiant company of the sweetest winter children of the sun. The blue sky had Sabbath and slept in its high dome, and down in its many mansions of *cañon* and cave, crystals grew in the calm nights, and fringed the rocks like mosses. The November torrents were soothed, and settled tranquillity beamed from every feature of rock and sky.

In the afternoon of December 16th, 1871, an immense crimson cloud grew up in solitary grandeur above Cathedral Rocks. It resembled a fungus, with a bulging base like a sequoia, a smooth, tapering stalk, and a round, bossy down-curled head like a mushroom—stalk, head, and root, in equal, glowing, half-transparent crimson: one of the most gorgeous and symmetrical clouds I ever beheld. Next morning, I looked eagerly at the weather, but all seemed tranquil; and whatever was being done in the deep places of the sky, little stir was visible below. An ill-defined dimness consumed the best of the sunbeams, and toward noon well-developed grayish clouds appeared, having a close, curly grain, like a bird's-eye maple. Late in the night some rain fell, which changed to snow, and, in the morning, about ten inches remained unmelted in the meadows, and was still falling—a fine, cordial snow-storm; but the end was not yet.

On the night of the 18th rain fell in torrents, but, as it had a temperature of 34° Fahrenheit, the snow-line was only a few feet above the meadows, and there was no promise of flood; yet

Photograph of John Muir in 1872. *Courtesy The Bancroft Library.*

sometime after eleven o'clock the temperature was suddenly raised by a south wind to 42°, carrying the snowline to the top of the wall and far beyond—out on the upper basins, perhaps, to the very summit of the range—and morning saw Yosemite in the glory of flood. Torrents of warm rain were washing the valley walls, and melting the upper snows of the surrounding mountains; and the liberated waters held jubilee. On both sides the Sentinel foamed a splendid cascade, and across the valley by the Three Brothers, down through the pine gorge, I could see fragments of an unaccountable outgush of snowy cascades. I ran for the open meadow, that I might hear and see the whole glowing circumference at once, but the tinkling brook was an un-fordable torrent, bearing down snow and bowlders like a giant. Farther up on the *débris* I discovered a place where the stream was broken up into three or four strips among the bowlders, where I crossed easily, and ran for the meadows. But, on emerging from the bordering bushes, I found them filled with green lakes, edged and islanded with floating snow. I had to keep along the *débris* as far as Hutchings' [hotel], where I crossed the river, and reached a wadable meadow in the midst of the most glorious congregation of water-falls ever laid bare to mortal eyes. Between Black's and Hutchings' there were ten snowy, majestic, loud-voiced cascades and falls; in the neighborhood of Glacier Point, six; from the Three Brothers to Yosemite Falls, nine; between Yosemite and Arch Falls, ten; between Washington Column and Mount Watkins, ten; on the slopes of South Dome, facing Mirror Lake, eight; on the shoulder of South Dome, facing the main valley, three. Fifty-six newborn falls occupying this upper end of the valley; besides a countless host of silvery-netted arteries gleaming everywhere! I did not go down to the Ribbon or Pohono; but in the whole valley there must have been upward of a hundred. As if inspired with some great water purpose, cascades and falls had come thronging, in Yosemite costume, from every grove and *cañon* of the mountains; and be it remembered, that these falls and cascades were not small, dainty, momentary gushes, but broad, noble-mannered water creations; sublime in all their attributes, and well worthy Yosemite rocks, shooting in arrowy foam from a height of near three thousand feet; the very smallest of which could be heard several miles away: a perfect storm of water-falls throbbing out their lives in one stupendous song. I have criticised [Thomas] Hill's painting for having two large falls' between the Sentinel and Cathedral rocks; now I would not be unbelieving against fifty. From my first stand-point on the meadow toward Lamon's only one fall is usually seen; now there are forty. A most glorious convention this of vocal waters—not remote and dim, as only half present, but with forms and voices wholly seen and felt, each throbbing out rays of beauty warm and palpable as those of the sun.

All who have seen Yosemite in summer will remember the comet forms of upper Yosemite Falls, and the laces of Nevada. In these waters of the jubilee, the lace tissue predominates; but there is also a plentiful mingling of arrowy comets. A cascade back of Black's is composed of two white shafts set against the dark wall about thirty feet apart, and filled in with chained and beaded gauzes of splendid pattern, among the living meshes of which the dark, purple granite is dimly seen. A little above Glacier Point there is a half-woven, half-divided web of cascades, with warp and woof so similar in song and in gestures, that they appear as one existence: living and rejoicing by the pulsings of one heart. The row of cascades between Washington Column and the Arch Falls are so closely side by side that they form an almost continuous sheet, and those about Indian Cañon and the Brothers are not a whit less noble. Tissiack is crowned with surpassing glory. Her sculptured walls and bosses and her great dome are nobly adorned with clouds and waters, and her thirteen cascades give her voice of song.

The upper Yosemite is queen of all these mountain waters; nevertheless, in the first half-day of jubilee, her voice was scarce heard. Ever since the coming of the first November storms, Yosemite has flowed with a constant stream, although far from being equal to the high water in May and June. About three o'clock this afternoon I heard a sudden crash and booming, mixed with heavy gaspings and rocky, angular explosions, and I ran out, sure that a rock-avalanche had started near the top of the wall, and hoping to see some of the huge blocks journeying down; but I quickly discovered that these craggy, sharp-angled notes belonged to the flood-wave of the upper fall. The great wave, gathered from many a glacier-*cañon* of the Hoffman spurs, had just arrived, sweeping logs and ice before it, and, plunging over the tremendous verge, was blended with the storm-notes of crowning grandeur.

During the whole two days of storm no idle, unconscious water appeared, and the clouds, and winds, and rocks were inspired with corresponding activity and life. Clouds rose hastily, upon some errand, to the very summit of the walls, with a single effort, and as suddenly returned; or, sweeping horizontally, near the ground, draggled long-bent streamers through the pine-tops; while others traveled up and down Indian Cañon, and overtopped the highest brows, then suddenly drooped and condensed, or, thinning to gauze, veiled half the valley, leaving here and there a summit looming along. These clouds, and the crooked cascades, raised the valley-rocks to double their usual height, for the eye, mounting from cloud to cloud, and from angle to angle upon the cascades, obtained a truer measure of their sublime stature.

The warm wind still poured in from the south, melting the snow far out on the highest mountains. Thermometer, at noon, 45°. The smaller streams of the valley edge are waning, by the slackening of the rain; but the far-reaching streams, coming in by the Tenaya, Nevada, and Illilouette *cañons* are still increasing. The Merced, in some places, overflows its banks, having risen at once from a shallow, prattling, ill-proportioned stream, to a deep, majestic river. The upper Yosemite is in full, gushing, throbbing glory of prime; still louder spring its shafts of song; still deeper grows the intense whiteness of its mingled meteors; fearlessly blow the winds among its dark, shadowy chambers, now softly bearing away the outside sprays, now swaying and bending the whole massive column. So sings Yosemite, with her hundred fellow-falls, to the trembling bushes, and solemn-waving pines, and winds, and clouds, and living, pulsing rocks—one stupendous unit of mountain power—one harmonious storm of mountain love.

On the third day the storm ceased. Frost killed the new falls;

the clouds are withered and empty; a score of light is drawn across the sky, and our chapter of flood is finished. Visions like these do not remain with us as mere maps and pictures—flat shadows cast upon our minds, too brighted, at times, when touched by association or will, to fade again from our view, like landscapes in the gloaming. They saturate every fibre of the body and soul, dwelling in us and with us, like holy spirits, through all of our after-deaths and after-lives.

Overland Monthly, 8 (April 1872): 347–60.

Among Muir's favorite places in the valley was "Sunnyside Bench," a narrow shelf on the cliffs, east of the upper Yosemite fall. He often retreated there to get away from the "crowds" and to record the Yosemite's moods and character. We give here the remarkable, mystical letter written to Mrs. Carr during one night spent among the waters of the fall.

New Sentinel Hotel*
Yosemite Valley, May 31, 1872

MIDNIGHT

O Mrs. Carr, that you could be here to mingle in this night moon glory! I am in the Upper Yosemite Falls and can hardly calm to write, but, from my thick baptism an hour ago, you have been so present that I must try to fix you a written thought.

In the afternoon I came up the mountain here with a blanket and a piece of bread to spend the night in prayer among the spouts of the fall. But now what can I say more than wish again that you might expose your soul to the rays of this heaven?

Silver from the moon illumines this glorious creation which we term falls and has laid a magnificent double prismatic bow at its base. The tissue of the falls is delicately filmed on the outside like the substance of spent clouds, and the stars shine dimly through it. In the solid shafted body of the falls is a vast number of passing caves, black and deep, with close white convolving spray for sills and shooting comet shoots above and down their sides like lime crystals in a cave, and every atom of the

---

* The letter was written on New Sentinel Hotel stationery but composed while on Sunnyside Bench.

magnificent being, from the thin silvery crest that does not dim the stars to the inner arrowy hardened shafts that strike onward like thunderbolts in sound and energy, all is life and spirit, every bolt and spray feels the hand of God. O the music that is blessing me now! The sun of last week has given the grandest notes of all the yearly anthem and they echo in every fibre of me.

I said that I was going to stop here until morning and pray a whole blessed night with the falls and the moon, but I am too wet and must go down. An hour or two ago I went out somehow on a little seam that extends along the wall behind the falls. I suppose I was in a trance, but I can positively say that I was in the body for it is sorely battered and wetted. As I was gazing past the thin edge of the fall and away through beneath the column to the brow of the rock, some heavy splashes of water struck me, driven hard against the wall. Suddenly I was darkened; down came a section of the outside tissue composed of spent comets. I crouched low, holding my breath, and, anchored to some angular flakes of rocks, took my baptism with moderately good faith. When I dared to look up after the swaying column admitted light, I pounced behind a piece of ice which was wedged tight in the wall, and I no longer feared being washed off, and steady moonbeams slanting past the arching meteors gave me confidence to escape to this snug place where McChesney and I slept one night, where I had a fire to dry my socks. The rock shelf extending behind the falls is about five hundred feet above the base of the fall on the perpendicular rock-face.

How little do we know of ourselves, of our profoundest attractions and repulsions, of our spiritual affinities! How interesting does man become, considered in his relations to the spirit of this rock and water! How significant does every atom of our world become amid the influences of those beings unseen, spiritual, angelic mountaineers that so throng these pure mansions of crystal foam and purple granite!

I cannot refrain from speaking to this little bush at my side and to the spray—drops that come to my paper and to the individual sands of the slope I am sitting upon. Ruskin says that the idea of foulness is essentially connected with what he calls dead unorganized matter. How cordially I disbelieve him tonight! and were he to dwell awhile among the powers of these mountains, he would forget all dictionary differences between the clean and the unclean and he would lose all memory and meaning of the diabolical, sin-begotten term, *foulness.*

Well, I must go down. I am disregarding all of the Doctor's physiology in sitting here in this universal moisture.

Farewell to you and to all the beings about us! I shall have a glorious walk down the mountains in this thin white light, over the open brows grayed with Selaginella and through the thick black shadow caves in the live oaks all stuck full of snowy lances of moonlight.

Muir, *Letters to a Friend*, pp. 119–23.

At the end of the summer Muir made his first trip north of the valley and into the great Tuolumne River Canyon and Hetch Hetchy Valley. He believed that the latter valley had also been created by glacial erosion, and his trip there was to find evidence to substantiate his theory.

This new research occupied nearly every hour of his day and he virtually ceased writing for publication. The delay worried Mrs. Carr, who cautioned him that others might begin stealing his ideas and publish them as their own—a fear already realized, actually, for in the spring and summer both Samuel Kneeland and Joseph Le Conte had presented papers on Yosemite's glaciers, taking most of their content from Muir's teachings yet giving him (or so Muir thought) too little of the credit.

To his mother Muir sent the following letter in which he reveals his joy that his scientific work has become clearly defined. It will be hard labor, he writes, but will give great reward.

Yosemite Valley
September 27th 1872

Dear Mother

I am just arrived from a long excursion up the great Tuolumne Cañon above Hetch Hetchy Valley. I did not complete my proposed work there, so I set out again tomorrow for two weeks more. I am measuring mtns & cañons with particular reference to mtn structure in connection with ice action. Also sketching waterfalls, special rock forms, etc.

I have just received a letter from Prof. Agassiz written by his wife. He regrets his inability to visit Yosemite & ramble with me among the old glacier works and ways. I could have enjoyed a visit with him in San Francisco but I could not spare the time. He may come another year.

I am able to do a great deal of very hard mountain exploration & someday will if I live tell you how mountains & river cañons & lake basins & meadows are made.

My life work is now before me plain enough & it is full of hard labor & abundant in all kinds of pure reward.

Nature-God asks much & gives much & if we only are pure in heart we will see him in all times, & in all lands.

I will write you again when I return. In the meantime once more farewell.

with love to all
Ever affectionately
Yrs. JOHN MUIR

Elizabeth I. Dixon, ed., "Some New John Muir Letters," *Southern California Quarterly* 46, no. 3 (September, 1964): 252–53.

The single most important scientific discovery Muir made during his explorations of the Yosemite high country took place in October 1871. While climbing toward the pass between Red Mountain and the Merced Peak (called Black Mountain in his day), high summits of the Clark Range, Muir noticed a silted stream whose source appeared to be a large field of snow. Suspecting that the silt was "glacial mud," he examined the ice field to discover the blue ice and *bergschrund* of a glacier: here was the "living glacier" which he had long sought and which he was sure would prove the validity of his glacial theories.

Mindful that his earlier thoughts on mountain structure had been appropriated by other scientists and presented as their own, Muir told no one of his remarkable find for fully one year. Mrs. Carr was the first to learn of it and, in Muir's words, the first to be given the "chance to steal."

Yosemite Valley
October 8th, 1872

Here we are again, and here is your letter of Sept. 24. I got down last evening, and boo! was I not weary after pushing through the rough upper half of the great Tuolumne Cañon? I have climbed more than twenty-four thousand feet in these ten days, three times to the top of the glacieret of Mt. Hoffman, and once to Mts. Lyell and McClure. I have bagged a quantity of Tuolumne rocks sufficient to build a dozen Yosemites; stripes of cascades longer than ever, lacy or smooth and white as pressed snow; a glacier basin with ten glassy lakes set all near together like eggs in a nest; then El Capitan and a couple of Tissiacks, cañons glorious with yellows and reds of mountain maple and aspen and honeysuckle and ash and new indescribable music immeasurable from strange waters and winds, and glaciers, too, flowing and grinding, alive as any on earth. Shall I pull you out some? Here is a clean, white-skinned glacier from the back of [Mt] McClure with glassy emerald flesh and singing crystal blood all bright and pure as a sky, yet handling mud and stone like a navvy, building moraines like a plodding Irishman. Here is a cascade two hundred feet wide, half a mile long, glancing this way and that, filled with bounce and dance and joyous hurrah, yet earnest as tempest, and singing like angels loose on a frolic from heaven; and here are more cascades and more, broad and flat like clouds and fringed like flowing hair, with occasional falls erect as pines, and lakes like glowing eyes; and here are visions and dreams, and a splendid set of ghosts, too many for ink and narrow paper.

I have not heard anything concerning LeConte's glacier lecture, but he seems to have drawn all he knows of Sierra glaciers and new theories concerning them so directly from here that I cannot think that he will claim discovery, etc. If he does, I will not be made poorer.

Professor Kneeland, Secretary Boston Institute of Technology, gathered some letters I sent to Runkle and that "Tribune" letter, and hashed them into a compost called a paper for the Boston Historical Society,* and gave me credit for all of the smaller sayings and doings and stole the broadest truth to himself. I have the proof-sheets of "The Paper" and will show them to you some time. But all such meanness can work no permanent evil to any one except the dealer.

As for the living "glaciers of the Sierras," here is what I have

* "On the Glaciers of the Yosemite Valley," *Proceedings of the Boston Society of Natural History* (Boston: Printed for the Society, 1872–1873), 15:36–47.

learned concerning them. You will have the first chance to steal, for I have just concluded my experiments on them for the season and have not yet cast them at any of the great professors, or presidents.

One of the yellow days of last October, when I was among the mountains of the "Merced Group," following the footprints of the ancient glaciers that once flowed grandly from their ample fountains, reading what I could of their history as written in moraines and cañons and lakes and carved rocks, I came upon a small stream that was carrying mud I had not before seen. In a calm place where the stream widened I collected some of this mud and observed that it was entirely mineral in composition and fine as flour, like the mud from a fine-grit grindstone. Before I had time to reason I said, Glacial mud, mountain meal.

Then I observed that this muddy stream issued from a bank of fresh quarried stones and dirt that was sixty or seventy feet in height. This I at once took to be a moraine. In climbing to the top of it I was struck with the steepness of its slope and with its raw, unsettled, plantless, newborn appearance. The slightest touch started blocks of red and black slate, followed by a rattling train of smaller stones and sand and a cloud of the dry dust of mud, the whole moraine being as free from lichens and weather stains as if dug from the mountain that very day.

When I had scrambled to the top of the moraine, I saw what seemed a huge snow-bank four or five hundred yards in length by half a mile in width. Imbedded in its stained and furrowed surface were stones and dirt like that of which the moraine was built. Dirt-stained lines curved across the snow-bank from side to side, and when I observed that these curved lines coincided with the curved moraine and that the stones and dirt were most abundant near the bottom of the bank, I shouted, "A living glacier." These bent dirt lines show that the ice is flowing in its different parts with unequal velocity, and these embedded stones are journeying down to be built into the moraine, and they gradually become more abundant as they approach the moraine because there the motion is slower.

On traversing my new-found glacier, I came to a crevass, down a wide and jagged portion of which I succeeded in making my way, and discovered that my so-called *snow-bank** was clear green ice, and, comparing the form of the basin which it occupied with similar adjacent basins that were empty, I was led to the opinion that this glacier was several hundred feet in depth.

Then I went to the "snow-banks" of Mts. Lyell and McClure and believed that they also were true glaciers and that a dozen other snow-banks seen from the summit of Mt. Lyell crouching in shadow were glaciers, living as any in the world and busily engaged in completing that vast work of mountain-making, accomplished by their giant relatives now dead, which, united and continuous, covered all the range from summit to sea like a sky.

I'm going to take your painter boys with me into one of my best sanctums on your recommendation for holiness.

Emerson sent me a profound little book styled "The Growth of the Mind," by Reed. Do you know it? It is full of the fountain truth.

I'm glad your boys are safely back. Perhaps Ned and I may try that Andes field together.

I would write to Mrs. Moores but will wait until she is better. Tell her the cascades and mountains of upper Hetch Hetchy [rest of sentence lost.]

I hope I may see you a few days soon. I had a pretty letter from Old Dr. Torrey, and from Gray I have heard three or four times. I am ever

Cordially
JOHN MUIR

Muir, *Letters to a Friend,* pp. 133–38.†

---

* Muir is alluding to a term used by Josiah Whitney and Clarence King to describe these areas of packed snow, which Muir here rightly calls "living glaciers."

† A longer, slightly differing version of this letter appears in William Frederic Badè, *The Life and Letters of John Muir,* 2 vols. (Boston: Houghton Mifflin, 1923–24), 1:334–52. This letter served as the basis for Muir's "Living Glaciers of California."

In October of 1872 Muir made the first recorded ascent of Mt. Ritter, one of the high eastern peaks of Yosemite. He took with him into this region three artists who had been sent to him by Carr, and while they remained in nearby Lyell Canyon, Muir made the climb alone. Years later he told of the ascent in his first book, *The Mountains of California* (1894), and we give here the most dramatic part of the chapter entitled "A Near View of the High Sierra."

This later narrative of Muir's contrasts vividly with his earlier Yosemite writings: less ecstatic, less personal, its very detachment displays his emergence as a writer. By the 1890s Muir had become a public figure. As a cofounder of the Sierra Club he was then concerned with shaping public opinion; in his articles and in this, his first book, he wished to endear readers to nature, to show there existed some moral value in the mountain experience. To accomplish this he sought everywhere to minimize his own role in his narratives; we find, for example, that the central figure in "A Near View of the High Sierra" is not Muir himself, but rather a mystical "other self," a detached and natural phenomenon over which he claims to have had no control. This literary tact is made all the more forceful because the reader is convinced of its honesty. The "other self" appears as a valid, if unexplainable, aspect of the human experience, and one which is most open to those daring to test nature's challenges. It is one more example of Muir's creative genius: to combine honesty of experience with honesty of expression.

This story of Ritter's climb is significant also in Muir's use of religious metaphor. Much of his Yosemite writing contained these metaphors, yet here they seem to reach a new level of intensity. At the very climax of this story of Ritter's conquest the reader will find the mountaineer assuming, at the most extreme moment of peril, the posture of Christ on the Cross, with "arms outspread"; yet the mountaineer is saved, by a force unexpected and beyond human understanding, and is led to a sort of terrestrial salvation. Seen in this light, the story is much more than an exciting account of mountaineering; it is a call to the public to come share the profound experience of the mountaineer, to view that at their base "Mountaineity and Christianity are streams from the same fountain,"* to understand ultimately that in the salvation of the mountains, and by implication all the environment, lies the salvation of each inhabitant of this planet.

It was now about the middle of October, the springtime of snow-flowers. The first winter-clouds had already bloomed, and the peaks were strewn with fresh crystals, without, however,

---

* From a letter written a few weeks after the Ritter climb to J. B. McChesney, January 10, 1873, in Badè, *Life and Letters*, 1:378.

affecting the climbing to any dangerous extent. And as the weather was still profoundly calm, and the distance to the foot of the mountain only a little more than a day, I felt that I was running no great risk of being storm-bound.

Mount Ritter is king of the mountains of the middle portion of the High Sierra, as Shasta of the north and Whitney of the south sections. Moreover, as far as I know, it had never been climbed. I had explored the adjacent wilderness summer after summer, but my studies thus far had never drawn me to the top of it. Its height above sea-level is about 13,300 feet, and it is fenced round by steeply inclined glaciers, and cañons of tremendous depth and ruggedness, which render it almost inaccessible. But difficulties of this kind only exhilarate the mountaineer.

Next morning, the artists went heartily to their work and I to mine. Former experiences had given good reason to know that passionate storms, invisible as yet, might be brooding in the calm sun-gold; therefore, before bidding farewell, I warned the artists not to be alarmed should I fail to appear before a week or ten days, and advised them, in case a snow-storm should set in, to keep up big fires and shelter themselves as best they could, and on no account to become frightened and attempt to seek their way back to Yosemite alone through the drifts.

My general plan was simply this: to scale the cañon wall, cross over to the eastern flank of the range, and then make my way southward to the northern spurs of Mount Ritter in compliance with the intervening topography; for to push on directly southward from camp through the innumerable peaks and pinnacles that adorn this portion of the axis of the range, however interesting, would take too much time, besides being extremely difficult and dangerous at this time of year. . . .

Icy Ritter was still miles away, but I could proceed no farther that night. I found a good camp-ground on the rim of a glacier basin about 11,000 feet above the sea. A small lake nestles in the bottom of it, from which I got water for my tea, and a storm-beaten thicket near by furnished abundance of resiny fire-wood. Somber peaks, hacked and shattered, circled half-way around the horizon, wearing a savage aspect in the gloaming, and a waterfall chanted solemnly across the lake on its way down from the foot of a glacier. The fall and the lake and the glacier were almost equally bare; while the scraggy pines anchored in the rock-fissures were so dwarfed and shorn by storm-winds that you might walk over their tops. In tone and aspect the scene was one of the most desolate I ever beheld. But the darkest scriptures of the mountains are illumined with bright passages of love that never fail to make themselves felt when one is alone.

I made my bed in a nook of the pine-thicket, where the branches were pressed and crinkled over-head like a roof, and bent down around the sides. These are the best bedchambers the high mountains afford—snug as squirrel-nests, well ventilated, full of spicy odors, and with plenty of wind-played needles to sing one asleep. I little expected company, but, creeping in through a low side-door, I found five or six birds nestling among the tassels. The night-wind began to blow soon after dark; at first only a gentle breathing, but increasing toward midnight to a rough gale that fell upon my leafy roof in ragged surges like a cascade, bearing wild sounds from the crags overhead. The waterfall sang in chorus, filling the old ice-fountain with its solemn roar, and seeming to increase in power as the night advanced—fit voice for such a landscape. I had to creep out many times to the fire during the night, for it was biting cold and I had no blankets. Gladly I welcomed the morning star. . . . After gaining a point about half-way to the top [of Ritter's cliff], I was suddenly brought to a dead stop, with arms outspread, clinging close to the face of the rock, unable to move hand or foot either up or down. My doom appeared fixed. I *must* fall. There would be a moment of bewilderment, and then a lifeless rumble down the one general precipice to the glacier below.

When this final danger flashed upon me, I became nerve-shaken for the first time since setting foot on the mountains, and my mind seemed to fill with a stifling smoke. But this terrible eclipse lasted only a moment, when life blazed forth again with preternatural clearness. I seemed suddenly to become possessed of a new sense. The other self, bygone experiences, Instinct, or Guardian Angel,—call it what you will,—came forward and assumed control. Then my trembling muscles became firm again, every rift and flaw in the rock was seen as through a microscope, and my limbs moved with a positiveness and precision with which I seemed to have nothing at all to do. Had I been borne aloft upon wings, my deliverance could not have been more complete.

John Muir, *The Mountains of California* (New York: Century, 1894), pp. 53–54, 57–58, 64–65.

By the winter of 1872–1873 Muir had emerged as a public figure, as a scientist and writer. Yet he was still an intensely private person, and so saw before him two equally appealing kinds of lives: the one public and exposed, the other more hermit-like, secluded with his own joyous discoveries.

Part Four closes with a journal entry which speaks of this dilemma. Muir addresses the need to make a choice of life's work through the apt image of a "weed of cultivation," a citizen plant which feels the need to revert to original wildness.

Some plants readily take on the forms and habits of society, but generally speaking soon return to primitive simplicity, and I, too, like a weed of cultivation feel a constant tendency to return to primitive wildness.

Well, perhaps I may yet become a proper cultivated plant, cease my wild wanderings, and form a so-called pillar or something in society, but if so, I must, like a revived Methodist, learn to love what I hate and to hate what I most intensely and devoutly love.

Linnie Marsh Wolfe, ed., *John of the Mountains: The Unpublished Journals of John Muir* (Boston: Houghton Mifflin, 1938), p. 90.

Part Five

Taking Leave (1873–1875)

Pine trees, granite, and water ouzels now. How true, and pure, and immortal they seem to me, yet somehow I feel satisfied to leave all and labor in other fields.

John Muir, Muir Papers, 1874

In the autumn of 1872 Muir journeyed to Oakland. He visited with the Carrs and with his new friend William Keith, the California landscape artist. He was taken to meet the editor of the *Overland Monthly* and was ferried back and forth across the bay, meeting members of the literary establishment to whom he was introduced as "the wild man of the woods."*

"Of social life and forms he knew nothing," Mrs. Carr later remembered. And Muir himself could stand the city turmoil for only two weeks. He fled to his Yosemite home and his studies. He believed he had much to do and he was in the process of working out the full implications of his glacial studies begun years before, but still not laid out in publishable form. So, during the year 1873, Muir was to fill hundreds of pages in notebooks and journals, make countless diagrams, sketches, and observations,† waiting until, as he finally wrote, "the entire series of phenomena has been weighed and referred to an all-unifying, all explaining law."‡ Perhaps he delayed also because of his belief, often stated in his private journals, that the most important lessons of wilderness were impossible to record in prose—the wordy explanations did little to make nature understandable.

We begin this part with several selections from Muir's journals. Some are dated, some are not, yet taken together they give insight into his thinking during this last year of residence in the valley, as does his subsequent letter to Mrs. Carr.

'What I have nobody wants.' Why should I take the trouble to coin my gold? If I should make an effort to show it, some will say it's fool's gold; no market, (Cannot be weighed on commercial scales) and if there was, I feel no inclination to sell. No standard; cannot use it, cannot be given away, much less sold. (A tree takes sunshine and grows; our souls take beauty, strive and grow, but neither the one nor the other may be used to warm and fructify others who keep away in shadow.) Cannot be taken; only some may be persuaded to come and see; it is like sunshine enjoyed which we may talk about, but cannot render

* From fragmentary notes made by Mrs. Carr in preparation for her article "John Muir," *California Magazine* (June 1892), found in Huntington Library, San Marino, California, File CA 40.

† Muir's explorations of the Kings–Kaweah–Kern regions are discussed, and his writings about the area anthologized, in Frederic R. Gunsky, *South of Yosemite: Selected Writings of John Muir* (Garden City, New York: Natural History Press, 1968).

‡ "Mountain Structure: Origin of Yosemite Valleys," *Overland Monthly* 12 (May 1894): 393–403.

available for warming others who choose or are compelled to sit in the shade.

Muir Papers, University of the Pacific, Stockton, California, File 37.17, "Autobiography," from the first page of the typescript copy of the "Hand-Sewn Notebook."

Sunnyside Bench
March 10. Before sunrise.
[1873]

This morning I rolled some bread and tea in a pair of blankets with some sugar and a tin cup and set off for my favorite Sunnyside Camp on the first bench of the north wall, east of the head of the lower Yosemite Fall, about five hundred feet above the level of the valley. It is a charming spot with abundance of water close at hand, a wild vineyard, fernery, and flower garden with picturesque groves of live-oak, Libocedrus, and pines, and views up and down the valley, while the interesting gorge between the upper and lower falls is near enough for sauntering to at one's leisure, and beside these advantages, it has an easy way out of the valley and up to the higher forests, by way of Indian Canyon. Birds, too, to keep one company, are here, and views of morning and evening lights and now and then noble storm scenes, with many of Nature's Yosemite extras thrown in from time to time. A' that and a' that and far more are the advantages of my Sunnyside Camp even in winter.

March 15 [?]

To ask me whether I could endure to live without friends is absurd. It is easy enough to live out of material sight of friends, but to live without human love is impossible. Quench love, and what is left of a man's life but the folding of a few jointed bones and square inches of flesh? Who would call that life?

Both the above journal entries from Linnie Marsh Wolfe, ed., *John of the Mountains: The Unpublished Journals of John Muir* (Boston: Houghton Mifflin, 1938; reprint ed., Madison: University of Wisconsin Press, 1979), pp. 120–21, 138.

If in after years I should do better in the way of exact research, then these lawless wanderings will not be without value as suggestive beginnings. . . These sweet free cumberless rovings will be as chinks & slits on life's horizon, through which I may obtain glimpses of the treasures that lie in God's wilds beyond my reach.

Muir Papers, File 19.4, Vol. 2, Yosemite, etc., 1870–1873, p. 58.

Yosemite Valley
March 30th [1873]

Dear Mrs. Carr:

Your two last are received. The package of letters was picked up by a man in the Valley. There was none from thee. I have Hetch Hetchy about ready. I did not intend that Tenaya ramble for publication, but you know what is better. *

I mean to write and send all kinds of game to you, with hides and feathers on, for if I wait until all becomes one it may be too long. As for LeConte's "Glaciers," they will not hurt mine, but hereafter I will say my thoughts to the public in any kind of words I chance to command, for I am sure they will be better expressed in this way than in any second-hand hash, however able. *

Oftentimes when I am free in the wilds I discover some rare beauty in lake or cataract or mountain form, and instantly seek to sketch it with my pencil, but the drawing is always enormously unlike the reality. So also in words sketches of the same beauties that are so living, so loving, so filled with warm God, there is the same infinite shortcoming. The few hard words make but a skeleton, fleshless, heartless, and when you read, the dead bony words rattle in one's teeth. Yet I will not the less endeavor to do my poor best, believing that even these dead bone-heaps called articles will occasionally contain hints to some

---

* The two pieces, mentioned in Muir's letter to Mrs. Carr, later appeared as articles: "Hetch Hetchy Valley," *Overland Monthly* 11 (July 1873): 42–50; and "A Geologist's Winter Walk," *Overland Monthly* 10 (April 1873): 355–58, reprinted in Part IV of this volume.

* Muir refers to Joseph Le Conte, "On Some of the Ancient Glaciers of the Sierras," read before the California Academy of Science, September 16, 1872; reprinted in *The American Journal of Science and Arts* 5, 3rd ser. (May 1873): 21ff.

living souls who know how to find them. I have not received Dr. Stebbin's letter. Give him and all my friends love from me. I sent Harry Edwards the butterflies I had lost. Did he get them?

Farewell, dear, dear, spiritual mother. Heaven repay your everlasting love.

JOHN MUIR

William Frederic Badè, *The Life and Letters of John Muir*, 2 vols. (Boston: Houghton Mifflin, 1923–24), 1:381–83.

First sent to Mrs. Carr, the following letter was forwarded to the *Overland Monthly* and published as "A Geologist's Winter Walk." An explanatory note to readers printed on the opening page outlined the circumstances which brought this, and other of Muir's articles, to the *Overland:* "The friend [Mrs. Carr] with whom Mr. Muir shares his mountain studies, one of many who know the untiring patience with which they are pursued, is well persuaded that the readers of "Living Glaciers," "Yosemite Valley in Flood," and other papers which have appeared, in the *Overland,* will enjoy these unprepared letter-pages, warm from the pen of the writer, and takes the responsibility of their publication." The article has remained more or less unknown since its first appearance, and we rescue it here, complete, in order to give a final example of Muir's discursive intelligence at work.

The article displays a narrative ascent from the city to the foothills to the Yosemite Valley, and then to the back country by way of Tenaya Canyon; a linking of intense vision and tremendous activity, where Muir's active experience in wild nature seems to be more important than any glacier or scientific theories which might result from his excursion. The piece begins with a moralized account of Muir's only dangerous fall in the mountains: he sees the cause in the influence of the city, whose "dead pavements" and "town fog" have blurred his wilderness thinking, his sense of his true self. Thereafter, the further he goes into the mountains the further he penetrates into the freedom of his own identity. By the end the narrative has accelerated; Muir is literally running in quest of mountain experience, the only lasting wealth.

As usual, the rocks of Yosemite, with their "granite flesh," are talkative and loving, treated as persons. Yosemite Valley is imaged as a temple: we even have the fine typical image of Muir in praying position on frozen lake Tenaya, "with my face close to the ice, through which the sunbeams were pouring," looking as six-rayed water-flowers. Even in this early article, the action and scale of wilderness are constant implicit commentary on the rest of earth, which has been turned into city within Muir's own generation, "seared with trade; bleared, smeared with toil; / And wears man's smudge and shares man's smell": Muir, like his exact contemporary, the poet Gerard Manley Hopkins, will affirm by enactive description that "for all this, nature is never spent; / There lives the dearest freshness deep down things" ("God's Grandeur"). The purpose of these descriptions is precisely to subsume self and to call attention to precious objects of concern, which offer to us our best impulses that we may read them. One annihilates the self, in truth, in order to read the signs which show the earth benevolent and teacherly, the earth as in itself the ultimate satire upon technology and greed.

In a letter of 1874, quoted in full below, Muir said: "I am hopelessly and forever a mountaineer. . . . Civilization and fever and all the morbidness that has been hooted at me have not dimmed my glacial eye, and I care to live only to entice people to look at Nature's loveliness. My own special self is nothing." The years of wandering in wild Yosemite, beginning to be absorbed by a man of such a character, at just that time in history, were working to form a new identity. It was an identity no longer merely ecstatic and scientific, but also and primarily ethical.

In the 1870s this was something new in the world. Nobody suspected it at the time, of course, but the development of one man's selfless self was in fact the genesis of the American conservation movement. Occasionally it happens thus, and one life history puts a stamp on focal aspects of a whole historical era. Muir was to leave the valley, marry and farm, moving even further toward the margins of his society in the 1880s, only to emerge in the nineties as writer and wilderness advocate, obviously at the center of certain crucial issues in the public sphere. "A Geologist's Winter Walk" will be read differently if one sees in it everywhere the ethical issues behind the images of intense joy.

A Geologist's Winter Walk

After reaching Turlock, I sped afoot over the stubble-fields and through miles of brown *Hemizonia* and purple *Erigeron,* to Hopeton, conscious of little more than that the town was behind and beneath me, and the mountains above and before me; on through the oaks and *chaparral* of the foothills to Coulterville; and then ascended the first great mountain step upon which grows the sugar pine. Here I slackened pace, for I drank the spicy, resiny wind, and was at home—never did pine trees seem so dear. How sweet their breath and their song, and how grandly they winnowed the sky. I tingled my fingers among their tassels, and rustled my feet among their brown needles and burrs.

When I reached the valley, all the rocks seemed talkative, and more lovable than ever. They are dear friends, and have warm blood gushing through their granite flesh; and I love them with a love intensified by long and close companionship. After I had bathed in the bright river, sauntered over the meadows, conversed with the domes, and played with the pines, I still felt muddy, and weary, and tainted with the sky of your streets; I determined, therefore, to run out to the higher temples. "The days are sunful," I said, "and though now winter, no great danger need be encountered, and a sudden storm will not block my return, if I am watchful."

The morning after this decision, I started up the Cañon of Tenaya, caring little about the quantity of bread I carried; for, I thought, a fast and a storm and a difficult cañon where just the medicine I required. When I passed Mirror Lake, I scarcely noticed it, for I was absorbed in the great Tissiack—her crown a mile away in the hushed azure; her purple drapery flowing in soft and graceful folds low as my feet, embroidered gloriously around with deep, shadowy forest. I have gazed on Tissiack a thousand times—in days of solemn storms, and when her form shone divine with jewels of winter, or was veiled in living clouds; I have heard her voice of winds, or snowy, tuneful waters; yet never did her soul reveal itself more impressively than now. I hung about her skirts, lingering timidly, till the glaciers compelled me to push up the cañon. This cañon is accessible only to determined mountaineers, and I was anxious to carry my barometer and clinometer through it, to obtain sections and altitudes. After I had passed the tall groves that stretch a mile above Mirror Lake, and scrambled around the Tenaya Fall, which is just at the head of the lake groves, and crept through the dense and spiny *chaparral* that plushes the roots of all the mountains here for miles, in warm, unbroken green, and was ascending a precipitous rock-front, where the foot-holds were good, when I suddenly stumbled, for the first time since I touched foot to Sierra rocks. After several involuntary somersaults, I became insensible, and when consciousness returned, I found myself wedged among short, stiff bushes, not injured in the slightest. Judging by the sun, I could not have been insensible very long; probably not a minute, possibly an hour; and I could not remember what made me fall, or where I had fallen from; but I saw that if I had rolled a little further, my mountain-climbing would have been finished. "There," said I, addressing my feet, to whose separate skill I had learned to trust night and day on any mountain, "that is what you get by intercourse with stupid town stairs, and dead pavements." I felt angry and worthless. I had not reached yet the difficult portion of the cañon, but I determined to guide my humbled body over the highest practicable precipices, in the most nerve-trying places I could find; for I was now fairly awake, and felt confident that the last town-fog had been shaken from both head and feet.

I camped at the mouth of a narrow gorge which is cut into the bottom of the main cañon, determined to take earnest exercise next day. No plush boughs did my ill-behaved bones receive that night, nor did my bumped head get any spicy cedar-plumes for pillow. I slept on a naked bowlder, and when I awoke all my nervous trembling was gone.

The gorged portion of the cañon, in which I spent all the next day, is about a mile and a half in length; and I passed the time very profitably in tracing the action of the forces that determine this peculiar bottom gorge, which is an abrupt, ragged-walled, narrow-throated cañon, formed in the bottom of the wide-mouthed, smooth, and beveled cañon. I will not stop now to tell you more; some day you may see it, like a shadowy line, from Cloud's Rest. In high water, the stream occupies all the bottom of the gorge, surging and chafing in glorious power from wall to wall, but the sound of the grinding was low as I entered the gorge, scarcely hoping to be able to pass through its entire length. By cool efforts, along glassy, ice-worn slopes, I reached the upper end in a little over a day, but was compelled to pass the second night in the gorge, and in the moonlight I wrote you this short pencil-letter in my notebook:—

"The moon is looking down into the cañon, and how marvelously the great rocks kindle in her light—every dome, and brow, and swelling boss touched by her white rays, glows as if lighted with snow. I am now only a mile from last night's camp; and have been climbing and sketching all day in this difficult but instructive gorge. It is formed in the bottom of the main cañon, among the roots of Cloud's Rest. It begins at the dead lake where

I camped last night, and ends a few hundred yards above, in another dead lake. The walls everywhere are craggy and vertical, and in some places they overlean. It is only from twenty to sixty feet wide, and not, though black and broken enough, the thin, crooked mouth of some mysterious abyss; for in many places I saw its solid, seamless floor. I am sitting on a big stone, against which the stream divides, and goes brawling by in rapids on both sides; half of my rock is white in the light, half in shadow. Looking from the opening jaws of this shadowy gorge, South Dome is immediately in front—high in the stars, her face turned from the moon, with the rest of her body gloriously muffled in waved folds of granite. On the left, cut from Cloud's Rest, by the lip of the gorge, are three magnificent rocks, sisters of the great South Dome. On the right is the massive, moonlit front of Mount Watkins, and between, low down in the furthest distance, is Sentinel Dome, girdled and darkened with forest. In the near foreground is the joyous creek, Tenaya, singing against bowlders that are white with the snow. Now, look back twenty yards, and you will see a water-fall, fair as a spirit; the moonlight just touches it, bringing it in relief against the deepest, dark background. A little to left, and a dozen steps this side of the fall, a flickering light marks my camp—and a precious camp it is. A huge, glacier-polished slab, in falling from the glassy flank of Cloud's Rest, happened to settle on edge against the wall of the gorge. I did not know that this slab was glacier-polished, until I lighted my fire. Judge of my delight. I think it was sent here by an earthquake. I wish I could take it down to the valley. It is about twelve feet square. Beneath this slab is the only place in this torrent-swept gorge where I have seen sand sufficient for a bed. I expected to sleep on the bowlders, for I spent most of the afternoon on the slippery wall of the cañon, endeavoring to get around this difficult part of the gorge, and was compelled to hasten down here for water before dark. I will sleep soundly on this sand; half of it is mica. Here, wonderful to behold, are a few green stems of prickly *Rubus,* and a tiny grass. They are here to meet us. Ay, even here, in this darksome gorge, "frightened and tormented" with raging torrents and choking avalanches of snow. Can it be? As if *Rubus* and the grass-leaf were not enough of God's tender prattle-words of love, which we so much need in these mighty temples of power, yonder in the "benmost bore" are two blessed *Adiantums*. Listen to them. How wholly infused with God is this one big word of love that we call the world! Good-night. Do you see the fire-glow on my ice-smoothed slab, and on my two ferns? And do you hear how sweet a sleep-song the fall and cascades are singing?"

The water-ground chips and knots that I found fastened between rocks, kept my fire alive all through the night, and I rose nerved and ready for another day of sketching and noting, and any form of climbing. I escaped from the gorge about noon, after accomplishing some of the most delicate feats of mountaineering I ever attempted; and here the cañon is all broadly open again—a dead lake, luxuriantly forested with pine, and spruce, and silver fir, and brown-trunked *Librocedrus*. The walls rise in Yosemite forms, and the stream comes down 700 feet, in a smooth brush of foam. This is a genuine Yosemite valley. It is about 2,000 feet above the level of Yosemite, and about 2,400 below Lake Tenaya. Lake Tenaya was frozen, and the ice was so clear and unruffled, that the mountains and the groves that looked upon it were reflected almost as perfectly as I ever beheld them in the calm evening mirrors of summer. At a little distance, it was difficult to believe the lake frozen at all; and when I walked out on it, cautiously stamping at short intervals to test the strength of the ice, I seemed to walk mysteriously, without any adequate faith, on the surface of the water. The ice was so transparent that I could see the beautifully wave-rippled, sandy bottom, and the scales of mica glinting back the down-pouring light. When I knelt down with my face close to the ice, through which clear sunshine were pouring, I was delighted to discover myriads of Tyndall's six-sided water flowers, magnificently colored. A grand old mountain mansion is this Tenaya region. In the glacier period, it was a *mer de glace,* far grander than the *mer de glace* of Switzerland, which is only about half a mile broad. The Tenaya *mer de glace* was not less than two miles broad, late in the glacier epoch, when all the principal dividing crests were bare; and its depth was not less than fifteen hundred feet. Ice-streams from Mounts Lyell and

Dana, and all the mountains between, and from the nearer Cathedral Peak, flowed hither, welded into one, and worked together. After accomplishing this Tenaya Lake basin, and all the splendidly sculptured rocks and mountains that surround and adorn it, and the great Tenaya Cañon, with its wealth of all that makes mountains sublime, they were welded with the vast South Lyell and Illilouette glaciers on one side, and with those of Hoffman of the other—thus forming a portion of a yet grander *mer de glace.*

Now your finger is raised admonishingly, and you say, "This letter-writing will not do." Therefore, I will not try to register my homeward ramblings; but since this letter is already so long, you must allow me to tell you of Cloud's Rest and Tissiack; then will I cast away my letter pen, and begin "Articles," rigid as granite and slow as glaciers.

I reached the Tenaya Cañon, on my way home, by coming in from the northeast, rambling down over the shoulders of Mount Watkins, touching bottom a mile above Mirror Lake. From thence home was but a saunter in the moonlight. After resting one day, and the weather continuing calm, I ran up over the left shoulder of South Dome, and down in front of its grand split face, to make some measurements; completed my work, climbed to the shoulder again, and struck off along the ridge for Cloud's Rest, and reached the topmost sprays of her sunny wave in ample time for sunset. Cloud's Rest is a thousand feet higher than Tissiack. It is a wavelike crest upon a ridge, which begins at Yosemite with Tissiack, and runs continuously eastward to the thicket of peaks and crests around [Lake] Tenaya. This lofty granite wall is bent this way and that by the restless and weariless action of glaciers, just as if it had been made of dough—semi-plastic, as Prof. Whitney would say. But the grand circumference of mountains and forests are coming from far and near, densing into one close assemblage; for the sun, their god and father, with love ineffable, is glowing a sunset farewell. Not one of all the assembled rocks or trees seemed remote. How impressively their faces shone with responsive love!

I ran home in the moonlight, with long, firm strides; for the sun-love made me strong. Down the junipers—down through the firs; now in jet-shadows, now in white light; over sandy moraines and bare, clanking rock; past the huge ghost of South Dome, rising weird through the firs—past glorious Nevada—past the groves of Illilouette—through the pines of the valley; frost crystals flashing all the sky beneath, as star-crystals on all the sky above. All of this big mountain-bread for one day! One of the rich, ripe days that enlarge one's life—so much of the sun upon one side of it, so much of the moon on the other.

Overland Monthly 10 (April 1873): 355–58.

In September Muir undertook his longest walking tour since the walk to the Gulf of 1867. With Galen Clark, artist Billy Simms (who painted the portrait found in this book), and with botanist William Kellogg, Muir proposed to visit the southern Sierra in order to gather data on his glacial theories, and to investigate the extent of the Sequoia groves. The letter below gives some idea of his plans, and of his intention to write his "first book."

Yosemite Valley
September 3rd, 1873

Dear Sister Sarah:

I have just returned from the longest and hardest trip I have ever made in the mountains, having been gone over five weeks. I am weary, but resting fast; sleepy, but sleeping deep and fast; hungry, but eating much. For two weeks I explored the glaciers of the summits east of here, sleeping among the snowy mountains without blankets and with but little to eat on account of its being so inaccessible. After my icy experiences it seems strange to be down here in so warm and flowery a climate.

I will soon be off again, determined to use all the season in prosecuting my researches—will go next to Kings River a hundred miles south, then to Lake Tahoe and adjacent mountains, and in winter work in Oakland with my pen.

The Scotch are slow, but some day I will have the results of my mountain studies in a form in which you all will be able to read and judge of them. In the mean time I write occasionally for the "Overland Monthly," but neither these magazine articles nor my first book will form any part of the scientific contribution I hope to make. . . . The mountains are calling and I must go, and I will work on while I can, studying incessantly.

My love to you all, David and the children and Mrs. Galloway who though shut out from sunshine yet dwells in Light. I will write again when I return from Kings River Cañon. The leaf sent me from China is for Cecelia.

Farewell, with love everlasting

JOHN MUIR

Badè, *Life and Letters*, 1:384–85.

The first entry in Muir's journal of this 1873 trip we give below. It is reproduced because it shows so well Muir's newly achieved ethical concerns: here we find the protest to the devastation being produced by grazing sheep herds, here he first condemns the destruction of the fragile Sierra meadows by the "hoofed locusts." Given Muir's future role in the conservation battles of the early twentieth century, the following brief paragraph might well be said to mark the moment he first realized that conservation would have to be made a matter of public policy.

Camp at Clark's Station
September 19, 1873

It is almost impossible to conceive of a devastation more universal than is produced among the plants of the Sierra by sheep. Clark's Meadows is fast changing from wet Carex to a sandy flat with sloping sides. The grass is eaten close and trodden until it resembles a corral, although the toughness of the sod preserves the roots from destruction. But where the soil is not preserved by a strong elastic sod, it is cut up and beaten to loose dust and every herbaceous plant is killed. Trees and bushes escape, but they appear to stand in a desert very different from the delicately planted forest floor which is gardened with flowers arranged in open separated groups. Nine-tenths of the whole surface of the Sierra has been swept by the scourge. It demands legislative interference.

Wolfe, ed., *John of the Mountains*, pp. 173–74.

Muir returned from his southern trip by way of the Owens Valley and Lake Tahoe. Evidently he thought he was now ready to write his long planned book on Sierra glaciers. He imposed upon himself a ten-month exile in Oakland, where he wrote some dozen articles, culminating in the technical "Studies in the Sierra," a seven-part magazine series explaining his theories about mountain structure and glacial erosion. It was consuming work, he later wrote, and it took its toll in broken health; yet he lingered on month after month until the task was finished.

One article written during this time was published in the *Overland Monthly* during September, 1874. In the first paragraph of this article, given here, Muir for the first time publicly discusses the harm done to the landscape by the "improvements" of the human settlers of the valley: ethical concerns are rapidly becoming central to his thinking and writing.

Twenty years ago, Yosemite Valley was a garden wilderness, as tenderly lovely as it is rocky and sublime, and much of its primeval beauty remains unimpaired. Its stupendous rocks poised themselves in the deep sky, scarcely more susceptible of human impress than the sun that bathes them. Its water-falls sing on unchanged, wild flowers bloom, and ferns unroll their fronds in many a sacred nook; but all its more accessible features have suffered "improvement." The plow is busy among its gardens, the axe among its groves, and the whole valley wears a weary, dusty aspect, as if it were a traveler new-arrived from a wasting journey. Lovers of clean mountain wilderness must therefore go up higher, into more inaccessible retreats among the summits of the range.

"By Ways of Yosemite Travel; Bloody Cañon," *Overland Monthly* 13 (September 1874): 267.

In September 1874, Muir ended the long stay in Oakland and headed once more for Yosemite. From the valley he wrote Mrs. Carr the two letters we have reproduced below. The first of these letters to his friend describes the "escape" from Oakland and his arrival in Yosemite where, for the first time in five years, he finds the rocks and trees "silent," and without lessons; Muir is coming to realize that the Yosemite years are over. (He would return, but never for the pure wandering of the last five years.) Before he left he wrote the wonderful "grasshopper letter" pictured and transcribed in his book. The second letter, we believe, is the last major statement written by Muir in this time of his emergence.

In it many of the personal, religious, and scientific themes of his wilderness thinking come together playfully, in a mature and distinctive style of writing.

Yosemite Valley
[September, 1874]

Dear Mrs. Carr:

Here again are pine trees, and the wind, and living rock and water! I've met two of my ouzels on one of the pebble ripples of the river where I used to be with them. Most of the meadow gardens are disenchanted and dead, yet I found a few mint spikes and asters and brave, sunful goldenrods and a patch of the tiny Mimulus that has two spots on each lip. The fragrance and the color and the form, and the whole spiritual expression of goldenrods are hopeful and strength-giving beyond any other flowers that I know. A single spike is sufficient to heal unbelief and melancholy.

On leaving Oakland I was so excited over my escape that, of course, I forgot and left all the accounts I was to collect. No wonder, and no matter. I'm beneath that grand old pine that I have heard so often in storms both at night and in the day. It sings grandly now, every needle sun-thrilled and shining and responding tunefully to the azure wind.

When I left I was in a dreamy exhausted daze. Yet from mere habit or instinct I tried to observe and study. From the car [train] window I watched the gradual transitions from muddy water, spongy tule, marsh and level field as we shot up the San Jose Valley, and marked as best I could the forms of the stream cañons as they opened to the plain and the outlines of the un-dulating hillocks and headlands between. Interest increased at every mile, until it seemed unbearable to be thrust so flyingly onward even towards the blessed Sierras. I will study them yet, free from time and wheels. When we turned suddenly and dashed into the narrow mouth of the Livermore pass I was looking out of the right side of the car. The window was closed on account of the cinders and smoke from the locomotive. All at once my eyes clasped a big hard rock not a hundred yards away, every line of which is strictly and out-spokenly glacial as any of the most alphabetic of the high and young Sierra. That one sure glacial word thrilled and overjoyed me more than you will ever believe. Town smokes and shadows had not dimmed my vision, for I had passed this glacial rock twice before without reading its meaning. . . .

Along the Merced divide to the ancient glacial lake-bowl of Crane's Flat, was ever fir or pine more perfect? What groves! What combinations of green and silver gray and glowing white of glinting sunbeams. Where is leaf or limb awanting, and is this the upshot of the so-called "mountain glooms" and mountain storms? If so, is Sierra forestry aught beside an outflow of Divine Love? These round-bottomed groves sweeping across the divide, and down whose sides our horses canter with accelerated speed, are the pathways of ancient ice-currents, and it is just where these crushing glaciers have borne down most heavily that the greatest loveliness of grove and forest appears.

A deep cañon filled with blue air now comes in view on the right. That is the valley of the Merced, and the highest rocks visible through the trees belong to the Yosemite Valley. More miles of glorious forest, then out into free light and down, down, down into the groves and meadows of Yosemite. Sierra sculpture in its entirety without the same study on the spot. No one of the rocks seems to call me now, nor any of the distant mountains. Surely this Merced and Tuolumne chapter of my life is done.

I have been out on the river bank with your letters. How good and wise they seem to be! You wrote better than you knew. Altogether they form a precious volume whose sentences are more intimately connected with my mountain work than any one will ever be able to appreciate. An ouzel came as I sat reading, alighting in the water with a delicate and graceful glint on his bosom. How pure is the morning light on the great gray wall, and how marvelous the subdued lights of the moon! The nights are wholly enchanting.

I will not try [to] tell the Valley [sic]. Yet I feel that I am a stranger here. I have been gathering you a handful of leaves. Show them to dear Keith and give some to Mrs. McChesney. They are probably the last of Yosemite that I will ever give you. I

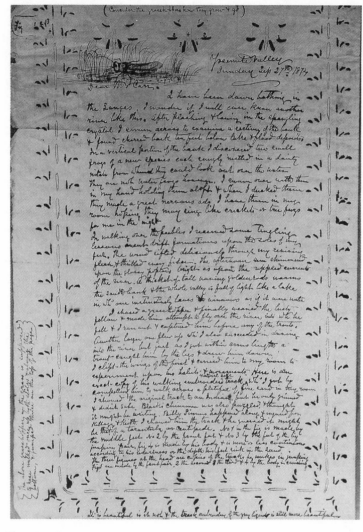

The "Grasshopper Letter," written to Mrs. Ezra S. Carr, September 27, 1874.
Reproduced by permission of The Huntington Library, San Marino, California.

will go out in a day or so. Farewell! I seem to be more really leaving you here than there. Keep these long pages, for they are a kind of memorandum of my walk after the strange Oakland epoch, and I may want to copy some of them when I have leisure.*

Remember me to my friends. I trust you are not now so sorely overladen. Good-night. Keep the goldenrod and yarrow. They are auld lang syne.

Ever lovingly yours

JOHN MUIR

Badè, *Life and Letters,* 2:10-12, 25-27.

(Consider the grasshoppers how they grow & go)

Yosemite Valley
Sunday Sep 27*th*, 1874

Dear Mrs. Carr,

I have been down bathing in the Ganges. I wonder if I will ever know another river like this. After plashing and laving in the spangling crystal I swam across to examine a section of the bank and found charred bark ten feet below lake and flood deposits. In a vertical portion of the bank I discovered two small frogs of a new species each snugly nestled in a dainty nitch from which they could look out over the water. They are not water frogs however. I swam over with them in my hand holding them aloft and when I ducked them they made a great nervous ado. I have them in my room hoping they may sing like crickets—or tree frogs for me in the night.

In walking over the pebbles I received some tingling lessons about drift formations upon the soles of my feet. The wind sifted deliciously through my reviving flesh, and thrilled every fiber. The afternoon sun shimmered upon the glossy poplars, bright as upon the rippled currents of the river. A thicket of tall waving golden rods warms the south bank and the whole valley is full of

* The original letter is considerably longer than the version given here. See William Frederic Badè, *The Life and Letters of John Muir,* 2 vols. (Boston: Houghton Mifflin, 1923-24), 2:10-27.

light like a lake in wh' one instinctively laves and winnows as if it were water.

I chased a grasshopper and finally wearied the lusty fellow and made him attempt to fly over the river into wh' he fell and I ran out and captured him before any of the trouts. Another larger one flew up wh' I also succeeded in driving into the river but just as I got within arms length a trout caught him by the legs and drew him down. I clipt the wings of the first and carried him to my room to experiment upon his habits and measurements. Here is an exact copy of his walking embroidered track (natural size) wh' I got by compelling him to walk across a plateful of fine sand in my room. I showed the original track to an Indian, but he only grinned and didn't sabe. Black's Chinaman was also puzzled and thought it might be writing. Billy Simms happened along and inquired for Kellogg and Keith. I showed him the track and he guessed it might be that of a tarantula or centipede. No. 1 in the fig[ure] is made by the middle feet. No. 2 by the front feet and No. 3 by the feet of the big jumping pair. Fig. 4 is made by his body and is more or less continuous according to his weariness or the depth his feet sink in the sand. The three figures at the head are copies of the tracks he mades in jumping. Fig. 1 are made by the front pair, 2 the second, 3 the third and 4 the body in crouching.

It is beautiful is it not and the track embroidery of the gray lizard is still more beautiful.

The above grasshopper in the grass is supposed to have walked once up both sides and along the bottom, and jumped thrice on the top of the page.

Quoted from Linnie Marsh Wolfe, *Son of the Wilderness: The Life of John Muir* (New York: Knopf, 1945; reprint ed., Madison: University of Wisconsin Press, 1978), facsimile between pp. 176–77; letter does not appear in the reprint.

The last letter we present is a famous one, and a fitting culmination to the story of this part of Muir's biography. From the book's perspective of Muir's emergence as scientist and writer, the key sentence is the one where he declares that his "glacial eye" is undimmed, and yet he resolves to go beyond study for his own development—to give himself to the task of interpreting wilderness for others: "I care only to entice people to look at Nature's loveliness." The last paragraph speaks of leaving Yosemite, and plans a travel schedule whose completion was to take up the next several years. So Muir leaves Yosemite, to return often again but never to return in the same way, as a student in the university of the wilderness.

Yosemite Valley
October 7th, 1874

Dear Mrs. Carr:

I expected to have been among the foothill drift long ago, but the mountains fairly seized me, and, ere I knew, I was up the Merced Cañon, where we were last year,* past Shadow and Merced lakes and our soda springs, etc. I returned last night. Had a glorious storm, and a thousand sacred beauties that seemed yet more and more divine. I camped four nights at Shadow Lake, at the old place in the pine thicket. I have ouzel tales to tell. I was alone and during the whole excursion, or period rather, was in a kind of calm incurable ecstasy. I am hopelessly and forever a mountaineer.

How glorious my studies seem, and how simple. I found out a noble truth concerning the Merced moraines that escaped me hitherto. Civilization and fever and all the morbidness that has been hooted at me has not dimmed my glacial eye, and I care to live only to entice people to look at Nature's loveliness. My own special self is nothing. My feet have recovered their cunning. I feel myself again.

Tell Keith the colors are coming to the groves. I leave Yosemite for over the mountains to Mono and Lake Tahoe in a week. Will be in Tahoe in a week, thence anywhere Shastaward, etc. I think I may be at Brownsville, Yuba County, where I may get a letter from you. I promised to call on Emily Pelton there. Mrs. Black has fairly mothered me. She will be down in a few weeks.

Farewell.

JOHN MUIR

Badè, *Life and Letters*, 2:28–29.

---

* Muir, Mrs. Carr, and several of his Oakland friends had camped in Yosemite and the Tuolumne region for several weeks during the summer of 1873.

The next several years were to be spent exploring other regions of the west, in climbing Mt. Shasta and in visiting some of the remote canyons of the southern Sierra. We close this composite autobiography with Muir's leave-taking from Yosemite, and present here some of the last notes he made while a valley resident. Taken together they give insight into his idea of the value of wilderness, learned while living in Yosemite, and into his own sense of self.

Escape the tyranny of custom and confusion and get cool and calm. [Escape] bad food and drink and air and be born again and make a new beginning.

Strange the faithless fuss made about taking a walk in the safest and pleasantest of all places, a wilderness. Even so fine a walker as Thoreau talks about the gruesome business of making wills, leaving father and mother, wife and child without hope of seeing them again, before setting out. Nobody can make a decent will without first taking a walk, cooling head, getting oriented, bathing head in the sky. Such self-conscious scarifying preparation would render one unfit for a walk in good wildness.

Muir Papers, File 37.14, Autobiographical Notebook, undated (1873?).

We seem to imagine that since Herod beheaded John the Baptist there is no longer any voice crying in the Wilderness. But no one in the wilderness can possibly make such a mistake. For every one of these is such a voice. No wilderness in the world is so desolate as to be without divine ministers. God's love covers all the earth as the sky covers it and also fills it in every pore, and this love has voices heard by all who have ears to hear. Everything breaks into love just as in the spring banks of snow burst forth in loud rejoicing streams.

Muir Papers, File 19.4, Vol. 2, Yosemite, etc. 1870–1873, p. 30.

As final text in this book we have chosen Muir's revealing and unanswerable question—"What is the human part of the mountain's destiny?" Only within the last century have our concepts of human time and geologic time coincided enough to permit us to ask, "How long will the mountains last if we express that in the days and years that measure man's survival?" So Muir's words focus on time's duration, but his emphasis is on the mountains rather than upon men. Muir is spokesman for earth that abides.

Photograph of Muir taken about 1910. *Courtesy The Bancroft Library.*

From 1875, when such questions as Muir's begin to be asked, we may perhaps date the intellectual origins of the American conservation movement. While Muir could not answer his own question about time and the duration of mountains, the question was always fundamental in his writing. But it was not so much a question to be answered in the formal way, as an issue to be lived and—splendidly—explored. Even though the answer did not show itself to him, Muir's work and example have made him inseparable from the human part of the mountain's destiny.

[1875]

Every sense is satisfied. For us there is no past, no future—we live only in the present and are full. No room for hungry hopes—none for regrets—none for exaltation—none for fears.

Enlarge sphere of ideas. The mind invigorated by the acquisition of new ideas. Flexibility, elasticity.

I often wonder what men will do with the mountains. That is, with their utilizable, destructable garments. Will he cut down all, and make ships and houses with the trees? If so, what will be the final and far upshot? Will human destruction, like those of Nature—fire, flood, and avalanche—work out a higher good, a finer beauty. Will a better civilization come, in accord with obvious nature, and all this wild beauty be set to human poetry? Another outpouring of lava or the coming of the glacial period could scarce wipe out the flowers and flowering shrubs more effectively than do the sheep. And what then is coming—what is the human part of the mountain's destiny?

Muir Papers, File 20.3, Notebook, June-September, 1875.

Selected Readings

Abbey, Edward. *The Journey Home: Some Words in Defense of the American West.* New York: Dutton, 1977. An extension of the most radical lines of Muir's conservationist thinking.

Badè, William Frederic. "John Muir in Yosemite." *Natural History* 20, no. 2 (1920): 121–41. Written while the editor was preparing *Life and Letters,* it describes Muir's life during 1869–1872.

———. *The Life and Letters of John Muir.* 2 vols. Boston: Houghton Mifflin, 1923–24. Badè was appointed literary executor and took eight years to complete this collection of letters.

Cohen, Michael P. "The Pathless Way: Style and Rhetoric in the Writing of John Muir." Ph.D. dissertation, University of California at Irvine, 1973.

Dixon, Elizabeth I., ed. "Some New John Muir Letters." *Southern California Quarterly* 46, no. 3 (September 1964): 239–58. The letters to Muir's brother Daniel are included, as is the one to his mother.

Doran, Jennie Elliott. *A Bibliography of John Muir.* San Francisco: Publications of the Sierra Club 51, 1916. Contains a reference list to John Muir's newspaper articles by Cornelius Beach Bradley.

Farquhar, Francis P. *Big Trees and the High Sierra.* Berkeley: University of California Press, 1948. Annotated Bibliography of literature on the history of the Sierra Nevada.

———. *History of the Sierra Nevada.* Berkeley: University of California Press, 1965. See especially the short account of Muir's Yosemite experience, Chapter 16.

Gunsky, Frederic R., ed. *South of Yosemite: Selected Writings of John Muir.* Garden City, New York: Natural History Press, 1968. Collection of Muir's writings about his trips to the southern Sierra Nevada after 1872; still the only convenient place to find material from Muir's *San Francisco Bulletin* articles.

Inventory of the John Muir Papers. Published by the Holt-Atherton Library, University of the Pacific, Stockton, California. Revised January-May 1976. The University of the Pacific has approximately 80 percent of all Muir's manuscripts.

John Muir Materials. Inventory of the John Muir holdings at the Yosemite Natural History Assocation Library, Yosemite, California, n.d.

Jones, Holway R. *John Muir and the Sierra Club: The Battle for Yosemite.* San Francisco: Sierra Club, 1964. The first extended attempt to fix Muir's place in the history of the Club, taking his story (and the Club's) from 1892 to 1914.

Kimes, William F., and Maymie B. Kimes. *John Muir: A Reading Bibliography.* Palo Alto: William P. Wrenden Books and Manuscripts, 1978.

Le Conte, Joseph. *A Journal of Ramblings through the High Sierra of California by the University Excursion Party 1875.* Reprint. San Francisco: Sierra Club, 1960. The 1870 journal on which this book is based is presumably lost.

Limbaugh, Ronald H. "The Muir Papers and the Intellectual Origins of Ecology." *Pacific Review* 4, no. 3 (Summer 1970): 4. A description of the Muir Papers at the Holt-Atherton Pacific Center for Western Studies, University of the Pacific, Stockton, California, written by the Center's archivist and librarian.

Matthes, François E. *The Incomparable Valley: A Geologic Interpretation of the Yosemite.* Berkeley: University of California Press, 1950. The best popular account of the geologic origins of the Sierra Nevada.

Matthiessen, F. O. *American Renaissance: Art and Expression in the Age of Emerson and Whitman.* New York: Oxford University Press, 1941.

Melham, Tom. *John Muir's Wild America.* Washington, D.C.: National Geographic Society, 1976. A popular and beautifully illustrated tribute to Muir.

Muir, John. *Studies in the Sierra.* Collected and edited by William E. Colby. San Francisco: Sierra Club, 1950. The articles about mountain structure first published in the *Overland Monthly,* May 1874–January 1875.

_____. *The Mountains of California*. New York: Century, 1894.
Reprint. Dunwoody, Georgia: Norman S. Berg, n.d.

_____. *The Yosemite*. New York: Century, 1912.

_____. *The Story of My Boyhood and Youth*. Boston: Atlantic
Monthly Co., 1913. Reprint. Madison: University of Wisconsin
Press, 1965.

_____. *Letters to a Friend: Written to Mrs. Ezra S. Carr, 1866–1879*.
Ed. William Frederic Badè. Boston: Houghton Mifflin, 1915. Reprint. Dunwoody, Georgia: Norman S. Berg, 1973.

_____. *A Thousand-Mile Walk to the Gulf*. Ed. William Frederic
Badè. Boston: Houghton Mifflin, 1916.

_____. *Steep Trails*. Ed. William Frederic Badè. Boston: Houghton
Mifflin, 1918.

Nash, Roderick. *Wilderness and the American Mind*. New Haven:
Yale University Press, 1967. Nash argues Muir's importance as
the "publicist" for the American conservation movement.

_____. "The Future of Wildness: A Problem Statement." *Bulletin of
the American Academy of Arts and Sciences* 3, no. 8 (May 1978):
18–24. A crucial statement on conservation issues.

_____. "Elder of the Tribe: Aldo Leopold." *Backpacker* 27, no. 6,
(June–July 1978). On the cultural importance of the wilderness in
the generations since Muir's death.

Roth, Hal. *Pathway in the Sky: The Story of the John Muir Trail*.
Berkeley: Howell-North Books, 1965. See the short account on
Muir and other early Sierra Nevada Mountaineers.

Sale, Roger. "On Being Not Good Enough." *College English* 34, no. 4
(January 1973): 500–510. Uses Muir as a touchstone for an extended metaphor that links the teaching of English to such concepts as the frontier and the wilderness.

Sargent, Shirley, *John Muir in Yosemite*. Yosemite, California: Flying
Spur Press, 1971. The popular account of Muir's Yosemite years,
with many fine illustrations and rare photos.

Shepard, Paul. *Man in the Landscape: A Historic View of the Esthetics
of Nature*. New York: Knopf, 1967.

Smith, Herbert Franklin. *John Muir*. New York: Twayne, 1965. An
account by a literary critic of many of the major writings.

Starr, Kevin. *Americans and the California Dream*. New York: Oxford
University Press, 1973. Especially useful for an account of California in the 1860s and 1870s.

Teale, Edwin Way, ed. *The Wilderness World of John Muir*. Boston:
Houghton Mifflin, 1954. A collection of excerpts taken from various published works.

Watkins, T. H., and Dewitt Jones. *John Muir's America*. Images of America Series. New York: Crown Publishers, 1976. A highly readable popular biography, with striking photographs of Yosemite.

Weber, Daniel B. "John Muir: The Function of Wilderness in an Individual Society." Ph.D. dissertation, University of Minnesota, 1964.

Wesling, Donald. "The Poetics of Description: John Muir and Ruskinian Descriptive Prose." *Prose Studies 1800–1900* 1, no. 1 (Fall 1977): 37–44.

Wolfe, Linnie Marsh, ed. *John of the Mountains: The Unpublished Journals of John Muir*. Boston: Houghton Mifflin, 1938. Reprint. Madison: University of Wisconsin Press, 1979.

_____. *Son of the Wilderness: The Life of John Muir*. New York: Knopf, 1945. Reprint. Madison: University of Wisconsin Press, 1978.

Yelverton, Thérèse [Viscountess Avonmore]. *Zanita: A Tale of the Yo-Semite*. New York: Hurd and Houghton, 1872. A novel about Muir in Yosemite, written by his contemporary.

Index